THE MINISTRY
WITHIN
How to Experience Ministry
from the Inside-Out

GP
GODZCHILD PUBLICATIONS

Published by Godzchild Publications
a division of Godzchild, Inc.
22 Halleck St., Newark, NJ 07104
www.godzchildproductions.net

Printed in the United States of America 2011— First Edition
Cover Design by Stephen Reid of Chosen Grfx

Library of Congress Cataloging-in-Publications Data The Ministry Within: How to Experience Ministry from the Inside-Out/Dr. Saundra Wall Williams.

ISBN 978-1-937095-19-2 (pbk.)

1. Williams, Dr. Saundra Wall. 2. Women 3. Christianity 4. Spiritual Growth 5. Leadership Development

Unless otherwise indicated, Scripture quotations are from the King James Version. All rights reserved.

Scripture quotations marked NKJV are from the New King James Version of the Bible. Copyright © 1979, 1980, 1982 by Thomas Nelson, Inc. All rights reserved.

Scripture quotations marked AMP are from the Amplified® Bible. Copyright © 1954, 1958, 1962, 1964, 1965, 1987 by the Lockman Foundation. Used by permission (www.Lockman.org). All rights reserved.

Scripture quotations marked The Message are from The Message Translation. Copyright (1993, 1994, 1995, 1996, 2000, 2001, 2002. Used by permission of NavPress Publishing Group. All rights reserved.

Table of Contents

DEDICATION

This book, *The Ministry Within*, is dedicated to my Lord and Savior Jesus Christ. He is all things in my life, my provider, my protector, my healer, and my teacher. When I think about what He endured so that I would not be lost, all I can do is to fall to my knees in thankfulness and worship. Everything I need to write - strength, courage, commitment and love came from above.

This book, *The Ministry Within*, is lovingly dedicated to my wonderful man of God, Dennis O. Williams. For the twenty-one years of our married life, Dennis has been a rock for me. He has served God and has been the head of our home. He has pushed me to be what God has called me to be and to do it in an excellent way. I can truly say that had it not been for the Lord on my side and the Lord giving me this mighty man of valor, this book would have never come forth. Dennis, I love you so much. The past twenty-one have been great, but I know the best is yet to come!

This book, *The Ministry Within*, is dedicated to our blessing from above – our son – Bradley Joseph Williams. When God blessed us with you as our son, a love entered my heart that I had not experienced. You are my sunshine. You are the joy of my heart. You understand that God has called Daddy and Mommy to do work to help others. Thank you for all the work you do when I have to go preach and teach. You are a great son! I love you and I am so proud of you!

My love and appreciation goes out to my family for all their love, support, prayers and encouragement: My parents, Mr. Leon Wall, Sr. and Mother Pauline Patterson Wall; my brothers, Leon Wall, Jr. and Robert Leon Martin; my nieces and nephews: Lexus, Kieonna, Zacc, Drew, Akyia, Nyla and Jorden; my grandmother, Mrs. Lillie Covington Wall (who all her life has been my great example of faith in God); my in-laws, Evangelist Augusta Williams and the late Dr. Dennis J. Williams; and the Wall, Patterson and Williams families. I love you all so much. God has truly blessed me to be a part of the best families in the world!

FOREWORD

There are a plethora of books on the market today that endeavor to explain, with some measure of tangible clarity, how to know you are called to ministry, the impact of the call, and how to proceed in developing and fulfilling that call of God upon your life. The work of ministry is not easy. It takes perseverance and endurance. Many outside the call view ministry work as a glamorous vocation having no idea of the trials and tribulations ministers have to endure for the call and subsequent privilege to preach and teach the word of God.

Dr. Saundra Wall Williams has penned such a book for those who have embraced their calling and find themselves thrust on the front lines of a spiritual battle without understanding why or knowing what to do in order to endure these trials and tribulations. Dr. Williams explains transformation of character through the transparency of her ministerial experiences. As a pastor of forty plus years my only regret is that I did not have such a book to read in my formative years.

The Ministry Within is a must read for new laborers as well as season clergy. I urge church leaders to secure a copy of this book for those God has positioned under their tutorage.

Bishop L. Foday Farrar
Bishop, Global Ministry,
Full Gospel Baptist Church Fellowship International
Pastor, Solid Rock Ministry International,
Garner, North Carolina

Introduction

For as long as I can remember, the fourth Sunday in August has always been the start of the annual revival at Philadelphia United Methodist Church in Rockingham, North Carolina. For many years as a child, teenager, and young adult I would sit in the pew in anticipation to hear the Word from the guest preacher. I would have never thought that one day I would be that guest preacher!

As the pastor of the church completed the introduction, she turned to me and she said with a loud shout – "Woman of God, Preach the Word!"

As my ears resounded with her voice, I immediately felt a charge to preach the gospel as I never had before. There suddenly came upon me a sense of urgency to get out of my mouth the words God had placed in my heart to bring to the people on that day. I felt anxious as the choir finished its pre-sermon hymn. That day, my sermon focused on the fact that we must never forget the power in the name of Jesus Christ. After completing the sermon, I knew that God had used me to speak His Word to His people.

Paul charged Timothy in 2 Timothy 4:2 with these words:
"Preach the word! Be ready in season and out of season. Convince, rebuke, exhort, with all longsuffering and teaching."

When I accepted the call into the Gospel ministry in

1996, I like Timothy, I had been charged to preach the Word. I knew that the calling of God on my life was that of Teacher. God had given me a vision for ministry. But before the vision could begin even in its conceptual stage, there had to be a preparation process for me. Although I was taught how to prepare sermons, how to visit the sick, and how to attend to the grieving, no one ever told me that I had to be "prepared" to endure the cost for ministry. No one taught me that this preparation included tests, trials, and tribulation.

My preparation for preaching and teaching the gospel is a continuous process. It began with me in my mother's womb (Jeremiah 1:5) and it continues to this present day. It has been a series of trials and testing of my faith. There were even times when I was broken. This brokenness was a higher level of testing that today I am thankful for.

I realized on that hot August day at Philadelphia United Methodist Church that all the tests, trials, and brokenness were worth it so that I could preach His Word to His people.

When I arrived at my home later that afternoon, I began to meditate on the phrase "And in all your getting, get understanding" (Proverbs 4:7). I realized that this understanding of the spiritual preparation for the call to ministry was critical for my growth process as a woman called to preach the word.

As a woman called to the gospel ministry, I was getting a lot of advice. People were very helpful; but, nothing could take the place of the experiences I have had as a part of my preparation process.

My desire is that someone would have written this type of book long ago. Then maybe I would have been better prepared for ministry – especially the ministry that would take place within me.

The purpose of this book is to encourage and equip women to walk confidently in your ministry calling and how to become a good steward of your call. These things cannot happen unless there is first a ministry within.

The documentation of these principles in this book is what I have learned about ministry up to this point in my life. I have learned these through experience, spiritual relationships with friends and mentors, teachings and preaching. But the majority I learned through my personal trials and tribulations of ministry.

Reading this book will help you with your own spiritual journey. Always know that the ministry within is real, personal and cannot be avoided.

CHAPTER ONE

❧

What does it mean to minister in season and out of season?

One day over lunch, I told a good friend that I was called into the gospel ministry to preach and to teach. She responded with a lot of tips. First, she me told how wonderful it was to be in ministry (she was a minister herself). She told me about the clothes I would have to purchase (the collar, the clergy apparel, etc.), and she even told me how to construct my initial sermon. But what she did not tell me was the amount of trials I would endure and encounter because of this call to ministry (Romans 5:3). She neglected to forewarn me about the whole picture. So, like any new minister "on fire for the Lord," I left that luncheon feeling excited!

I now know that my excitement should have been coupled with a bit of apprehension. I should have been more concerned about what I did not know and less concerned about the things I had to do. As one called to ministry, I was about to experience things in my life that were essential for my spiritual growth, but I was not equipped with the spiritual rigor to handle these experiences. I realized, very early in ministry, that ministry is not easy. On the outside, the work looks glamorous and fun. Ministers are constantly in the limelight, and it appears to be easy and breezy. In public, people carry this perception of perfection about ministers, namely that ministers are "next to God in our actions and thoughts." But in reality, ministers are human beings, too. We are normal people just like everyone else. We have emotional, spiritual, physical, financial and mental issues like everyone else. And yet, we are expected to do ministry in spite of ourselves.

So I had a lot to learn. I had a lot of questions to bring to God. I asked myself things like:

- *Why would God choose me for ministry if I have so many issues?*
- *Should not God work on me first?*
- *Should not God perfect my weaknesses, then call me to ministry when I am ready?*
- *Do I really want to be ready for ministry?*
- *Do I really want God to work on me to prepare for ministry?*
- *Do I really want God to perfect my weaknesses?*
- *All of these questions went through my mind. But before I could answer them, I had to decide if I was truly ready to do the work of ministry in season and out of the season.*

❧

IN SEASON AND OUT OF SEASON DEFINED

Paul challenges Timothy to do the work of the ministry when he writes "Preach the word; be instant in season, out of season; reprove, rebuke, exhort with all long suffering and doctrine" (2 Timothy 4:2). It is here that Paul writes what Timothy must do (preach the word), how Timothy must do it, and when and where the word must be preached. Paul is essentially preparing Timothy for everything that pertains to ministry. As part of Paul's preparation instructions, he tells Timothy to minister "in season, out of season."

If someone wants to properly prepare for ministry, they must first examine these two essential categories – "in season, out of season." To minister "in season" is the easier of the two. When you are in season, it means that times are good. It seems like everything is favorable and God's blessings appear to be upon everything you do. There are no hindrances or obstacles for you during "in season." Out of season ministry, on the other hand, is challenging work. When you minister, "out of season" you will preach the word regardless of your circumstances. You will preach and teach whether you have opportunity or not. You may experience trials, suffering, grief or any number of things that would impact you spiritually and/or emotionally. However, like Timothy, we must ready, prepared, available, and eager to preach and teach whether the time is favorable or not.

I like the way Dave Kistler, President of H.O.P.E. International Ministries describes in season, out of season. He states, "the preacher is to declare the word at both 'seasonable' times and 'unseasonable' times. 'In season' times are the ministry opportunities we TAKE. 'Out of season' times are the ministry opportunities we MAKE." Opportunities we take are those that are given to us, such as ministering on Sunday morning. These are in season. Opportunities we make are those that include sharing the gospel when it is uncomfortable (even though you know it is necessary), or times when you must encourage someone when, the truth is, you need encouragement yourself.

Let me give you a personal in season and out of season example. I often get calls to teach from pastors or leaders of women's ministries. These are in season. They are scheduled and planned. The audience is ready to receive and I am ready to minister. A specific out of season experience for me occurred when I was asked to help someone with a writing project that they were doing. I helped them, but in all actuality, I was behind schedule in the writing of my own book!

To do ministry in season and out of season means that you will operate in your call regardless of your personal circumstances. To endure the work of ministry, you must be prepared for every period in life.

L♥

The "Real" Work of Ministry

Trust me, ministry (if done well) can be a spiritually, emotionally, physically, and mentally draining task. But when I feel most drained, I now understand the whole picture. The big picture is this: Whatever God has called you to do, it is ultimately for the purposes of bringing Him glory and expanding His kingdom. It has nothing to do with you. You are just a vessel who is called to carry His ministry out. God doesn't really *need* us, but He *chooses* us because He *loves* us. When we realize this—that our purpose has absolutely nothing to do with us—then our focus will be on God.

Carrying out God's purpose in us will require spiritual maturity. When we allow growth to mature us so that we can carry out His purpose, we must get ready for tribulation. There is no other way to grow and mature spiritually. Spiritual growth only comes from our experiences with adversity. Expect hardship, suffering, and conditions that you feel are difficult to endure. Expect trials that test your faith. Expect to endure affliction. The "real" work of ministry cannot be taught, it can only be experienced through hardship, tests, and afflictions that you will experience. You discover the "real" work of ministry when you change on the inside so that you can carry out the call God has on your life. The work of ministry will require God to do a "real" work in you. His work in you renovates your heart. You experience the "real" work of ministry when your circumstances seem unbearable, yet you still have joy. You experience the "real" work of ministry when your best friend dies of cancer and you are left to minister to her three adult children. Yes, the "real" work of ministry happens when you experience personally that which you are called to preach and teach to others publically.

This is the "real" work of ministry (behind-the-scenes) that God requires if I am serious about what God has called me to do. The longer I am in ministry, the more I understand the statement Paul made to Timothy in 2 Timothy 2:3. Paul says, "You therefore must endure hardship as a good soldier of Jesus Christ." We will discuss the tests that God sends to improve us in subsequent chapters, but for now, let us have comfort in the words of James: "Count it all joy when you fall into various trials" (James 1:2)." Whether in season or out of season, count it all joy. As a minister, I have had my share of personal hardships, trials and tests. But the tests that have impacted me the most were all spiritual. I count it all joy. Why? Because those hardships transformed me from the inside-out. Those were the lessons that God used to prepare my heart for ministry. Hardships transformed my inner man. I count it all joy. God literally renovated my heart, changed my thought pattern and as a result, my desires and actions changed.

The work of ministry is 24-7. It never ends. And if ministry doesn't end, then I have always wondered if the tests will ever end? To date, I have not received an answer to that question, but I will tell you this: when you answer the call and live out what God requires of you, He gives you the strength to endure more tests, more afflictions and more hardships. No matter what your "ministry" is, if you are called to it, and you have a desire to walk in that call, you must prepare for an inner battle. The real work of ministry must happen on the inside of the minister. Once you have learned what it means to endure afflictions, then God will release you and empower you to do the work of your call and fulfill your ministry (2 Timothy 4:5). No one can tell you what your afflictions will be or what trials you will have to endure before, during and after the call. But know that the tests will come. How we respond to those tests and trials will determine if we are ready for ministry in season and out of season.

PREPARING FOR BATTLE

You may ask the question, "Why must I fight or experience pain because of something that God has called me to do?" Why must I prepare for battle at all? The common misunderstanding about ministry is that once we surrender to God, our trials will disappear. It all gets easier and the minister never has to go through anything. But this is completely untrue! Remember, God has called you. And because God has called you, the devil wants to destroy you! This is why we must prepare for battle.

1 Peter 5:8 Be sober, be vigilant; because your adversary the devil, walks about like a roaring lion, seeking whom he may devour:

When you answered the call of God on your life, you signed up for combat and war! You did not sign up to sit passively and listen haphazardly to the instructions of a boring teacher. No, you signed up to participate in tearing down the kingdom of darkness and lifting up the name of Jesus at all costs. No one signs up for combat without expecting to experience some level of pain. You must serve in spite of the pain. You must serve in spite of the suffering. As a minister, you must be able to endure the sadness and grief of your own circumstances while at the same time, celebrate the move of God in others.

The Devil is not playing with us. He not only wants to destroy you as an individual, but he wants to destroy the ministry that God has placed inside of you. Regardless of the magnitude of God's call on your life, people will be impacted. The Devil, therefore, does not want those people to hear what God has to say through you. So, he is constantly and consistently attempting to destroy you and the ministry which God has placed inside of you.

Yes, God wants to use us for his purpose, whether for women, men, homeless people or whatever He's called us to, but still, God has to change us on the inside for the people He's called us to. The devil wants us to resist change by any means necessary. This is a constant battle. But there is another power within us that is at war with our mind. This power makes us a slave to the sin that is still within us. This war is what Paul calls "a war in our members" (Romans 7:23). But the good news is, the end reward is far greater than the beginning or middle (Romans 8:18). Trust me, if I had known that my call to women meant that I would go through what I went through just to experience other women's pain, I would've said "No, God! No! No! Give me something else!" Had I known what I know now, I don't think I would've accepted the call. But that's the genius of God. He exposes what we can handle because He knows our level of maturity throughout the various stages of our lives.

I thought I knew what it meant to be a minister in season and out of season. But I had some maturing to do. I had to experience some things on my own. I was taught to do the "things" of ministry—like communion, and baptism—but no one told me that something inside of me had to be developed. I knew how to go to the hospital to visit the sick or to conduct a funeral, but no one told me that I would be hurt; that friends would walk away from me as a result of making this decision to preach the gospel of Jesus Christ; that I would find myself alone more often than I would find myself in the company of people who would encourage me.

It was here in this moment of realization that God revealed to me...He needed to work on my character.

Character is who I am on the INSIDE. My character defines my heart and will determine my actions. Your character will determine not only how you do ministry, but it will define the ministry you will become. The work of God inside us through the Holy Spirit brings us to a place of spiritual maturity and preparation for ministry. Without Godly character inside you, there is no acceptable work of ministry outside of you.

℘

QUESTIONS FOR REFLECTION
When you said, "Yes" to the calling to do ministry, what were some initial impressions you had? Did you know what you were getting into? What has changed since that moment?

THINK ABOUT IT
If God exposed you to everything you would have to go through as a minister of the Gospel, would you have been willing to endure the hardships?

QUESTIONS FOR DISCUSSION
Have you experienced an "out of season" moment in ministry? What were the circumstances? How did you minister during that season? What has changed since then?

CHAPTER TWO

What does it mean to have character? Why is it important?

A few months ago, a woman who I considered my sister in Christ said something to me after church that I took issue with. It hurt me so bad that I started crying. The old nature began to rise. My first desire was to take off one of the red three-inch heel shoes I was wearing and beat her with it. That's how angry I was. I didn't get upset because she had lied on me, even though she had. I didn't break down because she was envious of me, even though she was. What truly hurt me was that she was using this situation to attack my character. I was under attack and I wanted to fight. It was all about my character. I knew the accusations weren't true and I knew that God would expose the truth eventually. But when the young lady said what she said to me, I didn't stop to think, "What would Jesus do?" My first reaction was "what is Saundra going to do?!"

I was headed in the wrong direction. I was about to react in a way that would not have pleased God. But thank God for friends! One of my friends went inside to get my husband as I continued to yell, scream, and cry. I felt extremely disrespected and I wanted someone to help me "physically fix" this problem! And then, all of a sudden, out the corner of my eye, I saw a young woman standing on the side. This young woman was assigned to me and I had been ministering to her for some time. I knew

God wanted me to minister to her from the first moment she walked into our church. She and I had spent hours together discussing how God was maturing her and how she desired to move forward with the call of God on her life. As I continued with my tirade, I could see the look on this young lady's face. It was a look of confusion and disappointment. Then I heard in my spirit, "You're getting ready to crucify your testimony." Immediately my spirit came into alignment. My original plan was to fuss one woman out. But God stopped me and showed me where my true focus was supposed to be. My true focus had to be on what He called me to do – regardless of my current situation.

The natural desire would've been to let anger overrule my spirit because I was so fed up. But that would have created a problem. At that moment, I needed to live out Galatians 2:20, "I have been crucified with Christ; it is no longer I who live, but Christ lives in me; and the life which I now live in the flesh I live by faith in the Son of God, who loved me and gave Himself for me. The Christ in me took over, and ultimately, the spirit of love won above my desire to retaliate. As I saw that other woman standing out in the distance, I realized that my testimony was more important than the words I wanted to exchange. I couldn't allow everything I had talked to the young woman about to be ruined because of one bad period of anger. I was about to damage the fruit that God has assigned me to bear. My prayer became: Lord, give me Your Character. Teach me what I need to do and help me to deny myself in order to have the character of Christ.

✒

CHARACTER DEFINED

Thomas Paine is considered one of the founding fathers of the United States. He describes character well when he said, "Reputation is what men and women think of us; character is what God and angels know of us." Our character is who we really are on the inside. It is what we do when no one is looking. Our character is determined by an accumulation of thoughts, values, words, and actions. These features of our character define who we are as a holistic being.

Our character will reveal what our hearts and minds are really like. Character is what God sees. The author of the Old Testament book of First Samuel writes about character in the Lord's description of David. In this scripture, the Lord said to Samuel, "Do not look at his appearance or his physical stature, because I have refused him. For the Lord does not see as man sees; for man looks at the outward appearance, but the Lord looks at the heart" (1 Samuel 16:7). Begin to reflect on the question, "When God looks at my heart, what does He see?" What God sees is our character. What we show others is our image. Unfortunately, we have become more entrenched with what men and women think of our image instead of spending time building our Christ-like character. We have become obsessed with maintaining a reputation. And a reputation in ministry is important; but we must remember that your ministerial character is even more crucial.

When I got home from that altercation in church, I realized, "if I would've crucified my testimony, God would've had to take me through so much more just so I could build my testimony back up." *I can't do what Saundra always wants to do. Why? Be-cause Christ wants to reveal himself in me at any cost.* This situation taught me two essential things about character. First, character development for ministry is a daily occurrence. Consider this verse:

Luke 9:23- And he said to them all, If any man will come after me, let him deny himself, and take up his cross daily, and follow me.

I will return to this verse to discuss self-denial, but the word to remember is "daily." When you say, "Yes" to the call into ministry, it requires a complete doing away of yourself on a daily basis. Not just on Sunday—but every day. Your life belongs to God. And not only that, your life also belongs to those whom God has called you to serve. If ministry is to be done "in season and out of season," then you must be willing to model the character of Christ on a daily basis.

There are many things that God will show us about our character every day. It could be something as small as a situation that doesn't go my way, or a sermon I preached that I now have to live out. Whatever the trial may be, I've learned that God teaches me a lesson about character for many reasons. It may not be for my immediate personal needs, but perhaps it is for present or future fruit - someone in my path to whom God needs me to minister. Thus, He's preparing me now for what is to come later. To this end, I have learned to carry out what Paul said to the church at Corinth: "I die daily" (2 Corinthians 15:31b). Now I must admit: dying daily is one of the most challenging things to live out. I am human; and there are times when I would just like to do what I would like to do when it comes to my thoughts, my will and my actions.

My pastor preaches all of the time, "to surrender ALL means to surrender EVERYTHING." To surrender everything means I must be willing to die to myself in order to bear fruit. Thus, the words from John 12:24 have become a part of my testimony, "Verily, verily, I say unto you, Except a corn of wheat fall into the ground and die, it abideth alone; but if it die, it bringeth forth much fruit."

Sometimes God will allow me to face issues today to prepare me for the ministry I must do for someone else later on. For example, in the past I have struggled with women who lived in abusive situations. I could not understand why a woman would continue to subject herself to abuse. My thought was, "Just walk away!" But God planted me in a situation where the woman was dealing with abuse. In order to speak life to her, I had to somewhat understand what she was going through emotionally. Immediately, God brought back to my mind a college relationship that I desperately wanted to get out of, but for some reason, I could not leave. I immediately had to ask myself, "Why couldn't I walk away? What kept me there?" My answers, although different than that woman in an abusive relationship, helped me to put myself in her shoes. Who would've thought that a hardship I had to endure over twenty years ago was helping to prepare me for ministry? Only God.

❦

LET GOD DEVELOP YOU FIRST!

The second lesson I learned from this situation is that ministers must develop the character of Christ before we can lead or help to develop the character of Christ in others. Do not assume that because you have been called into ministry that you already have the character of Christ. God is always working on who we are on the inside so that we can become more like Him. Our physical appearance is something that God appreciates but it is not God's focus. God wants to develop us from the inside. It's all about the heart of man. God wants to deal with our hearts. This is where He begins to change us, so that we can help others.

Many women are battling with many things—insecurity, distrust, and low self-esteem to name a few. But whenever I go through my own personal afflictions, God will always show me why I had to endure. I realize how crucial character is, so my prayers have now changed. My mindset has become, "God deal with me in whatever way you see fit so I can minister to those whom you've called me to." In times past, I used to have a problem with the statement "deal with me in whatever way you see fit." I would say it, but in my heart I did not want to be "dealt with." But growth in Christ, and being shaped and molded into the character of Christ gave me an assurance that God would perfect those things that concern me (Psalms 138:8).

Also know this. God often deals with us to develop our spirits in the character of Christ in order to show us that we are not ALL THAT! God has to make you humble. God knows what you need and allows some things to happen so that you never

decide to rely on your own strength. A small amount of development is a big thing in God's mind. From my personal experience, I
had to learn to "be quick to hear and slow to speak" (James 1:19).
People would often say things to me, and immediately I would
have a response. As I grew in the character of Christ, I learned
to be more silent. I now say, "I'm going to be in prayer with you
about that" instead of flying off at the mouth about something
that I know very little about. This was something that God had to
develop in me as it relates to my character.

Ⰲ

OUR ULTIMATE GOAL: TO BE LIKE CHRIST

Our character must be transformed daily. God must minister to
us about character before we try to minister to others. And ultimately, our number one goal is to be like Christ. That is the des-
tination address on our journey toward character development.
When we talk about being like Christ, we must first check our
heart. Make sure that your heart (and the things that go into
your heart) are Christ-like. God chose us before the foundation
of the world. He commands us to be holy and without blame before Him in love (Ephesians 1:4). We must prune away everything
that does not please God. If there is anything in your heart or
anything that is not like Christ, it must be dealt with and elimi-
nated. If your actions do not line up with God's word, and if you
are treating people poorly, then you are not reflecting the image
of Christ and your ministry does not please God.

Luke 9:23- And he said to them all, If any man will come after me, let him deny himself, and take up his cross daily, and follow me.

The Scripture appears again. This time, because we must remember the importance of self-denial. In order to be more like Christ, we must deny ourselves. That is what the Bible admonishes us to do. We must come down from ourselves. We must remain humble, teachable, honest, and repentant. As women in ministry, people may try to place you on a pedestal. They may aid in helping you think that you're all that; that you are more than you really are. But you must understand that God is everything. Learn to deny yourself of everything, which means that you literally put yourself in a place that recognizes: "I don't do anything without God." Until you get to that point, you won't be effective.

Many ministers are looking to their credentials, but credential with no character is like zeal with no knowledge; or knowledge with no integrity. Like 1 Corinthians 13:3 tells us, it profits us nothing. In reality, accolades won't help you if God isn't helping you. It is by his strength, knowledge and power that we are able to complete our assignment for his glory.

We must deny ourselves daily. God's character is obtained when we deny ourselves. A minister committed to self-denial realizes that her opinion doesn't matter if it doesn't match God's. In other words, if my outlook does not match the Word of God, then it does not matter. If I am counseling or ministering, I must deny what Saundra wants to say, and line my counsel up with the Word of God. My thoughts, actions, and everything that I want to do, although it may be important, will pale in comparison to what God wants for me. True character development means that we do not rely on our strength. In everything, we go to God because we understand that Christ is in control.

Walk away from this chapter knowing that character development is not a one-time event. Character development is an ongoing process where God teaches us to put our "being" (who we are) before our "doing" (what we do). Character is who we are on the INSIDE. Our character defines our heart and will determine our actions. Your character will determine not only how you do ministry, but it will define the ministry you will become. The work of God inside us through the Holy Spirit brings us to a place of spiritual maturity and preparation for ministry. Without Godly character inside of you, there is no acceptable work of ministry outside of you.

God has called us to do a work for His glory—a daily work of self-denial. God takes character seriously; therefore, we must live in full submission to God's will in order to be most effective. We may get angry, but we are not supposed to sin. When we find ourselves reacting like I did with the woman at my church, we need to focus our attention to the people watching us on the sidelines. Focus on the mission, not the distraction. Focus on God, and not your own opinion. The more we live in the character of God, the less we will have to go through. But the more we refuse to surrender to God, the more "going through" we'll have to do!

QUESTIONS FOR REFLECTION

When God examines your heart, what does He see? How much character building/growth have you experienced over the course of your ministerial call?

THINK ABOUT IT

Luke 9:23 is a tough verse to swallow. As you meditate on this passage, which words are most difficult to live out? Which is more difficult: to deny oneself or to do it daily? Why?

QUESTIONS FOR DISCUSSION

Has anyone ever attacked your character? How did you respond? Was God pleased with the way you handled the situation? How long did it take you to resolve the issue?

CHAPTER THREE
ℒ♥
How Does God Develop Our Character?

You have already read about the meaning of character and why character is crucial to the work God has called you to do. Remember, God wants to make us more like Jesus Christ. As a minister of the Gospel, our character qualifies us. Our character differentiates us from the world. The only way the world can see Christ in us is if we allow God to reveal the image of His son through us. This requires character development. This requires inner growth and transformation. Yes, even as a minister of the gospel.

Now you may be saying to yourself, "My character is already developed. I am a Christian. I have been called by God to preach! I have arrived. My job now is to help others." All this may be true, but again, if we are to help develop the character in others, we must concentrate on building our own first. The character traits of love, joy, peace, longsuffering, kindness, goodness, faithfulness, gentleness, and self-control (Galatians 5:22-23) must be continuously developed in us. Let me say it one more time: character development is not a one-time event. It is something that continues for a lifetime.

How does God develop our character?

As my Pastor would say, I'm so glad you asked. God develops our character by dealing with us, and God deals with us by taking us through various trials and tribulations. This is the focus of this chapter. Your trials and tribulations have a purpose. They are a test of your faith and a method to build your character. Our circumstances allow for our character to be tested and our faith to be exercised. When I talk about God dealing with us, I am talking about a church phrase commonly known as "going through." If I had to define "going through", I would reference James 1:2-4: "My brethren, count it all joy when you fall into various trials, knowing that the testing of your faith produces patience. But let patience have its perfect work, that you may be perfect and complete, lacking nothing" (NKJV). This scripture reveals several things about "going through." Most importantly, to "go through" means you are going to experience a trial or a tribulation. These trials to which James refers are persecutions. In his day, it was common for Christians to be persecuted. Those who claimed Jesus Christ as Savior could have had their homes destroyed. They could've been dragged off to prison by the local authorities, all because of their relationship with Jesus Christ. I thank God we do not face this kind of persecution for our belief in Christ (at least not in the United States), but notice the term "various trials" in the second verse. James had other trials in mind, also. Fights and quarrels with family members, disagreements with friends or coworkers, mental and physical sickness, issues with children, financial struggles, addictions, grief and marital problems; all of these are examples of "various trials." When God allows us to "go through," He is literally dealing with us *through* our circumstances so that we can become more like Him. He's developing our character so that the inside of us will be like Him. Our hope is that, in the end, the Fruit of the Spirit will become the character traits that people see in us.

What is God Growing When I am Going Through?

When I first gave my life to Christ, I realized very early in my journey that being a Christian did not make me immune to the trials of life. As a minister of the gospel, I have come to understand that "going through" is a critical process necessary for spiritual growth and maturity. Earlier we reviewed a definition for "going through" according to James 1:2-4. But the question still remains: *why* do we have to experience this? Why is this development necessary for ministry growth?

God's ultimate purpose for each of us is to grow (Romans 8:29). When we survive and overcome adversity, we grow. God sanctifies us for God's purposes. When your faith is tested by the trials you experience, you grow. 1 Peter 1:6-7 (NLT) explains testing this way:

"So be truly glad. There is a wonderful joy ahead, even though you have to endure many trials for a little while. These trials will show that your faith is genuine. It is being tested as fire tests and purifies gold – though your faith is far more precious than mere gold. So when your faith remains strong through many trials, it will bring you much praise and glory and honor on the day when Jesus Christ is revealed to the whole world."

Trials and tribulations develop our character. When our character is developed, we are able to rejoice in our suffering and adversities. Why would I want to rejoice in suffering? Because suffering produces perseverance, and perseverance produces character, and character produces hope (Romans 5:3-5). Adversity has a unique way of humbling us. And humility helps us to relate to others. It is all a circular process for character development. When you encounter adversity through trials and tribulations, it will make you *and* break you. It *makes* you in areas of spiritual development and personal growth In God. It breaks you in areas of spiritual pruning and uprooting. The making and breaking is a subject we will discuss in the next chapter. But right now, know this: your character in God will grow when you are in the middle of a severe trial. Don't run from the trials; embrace them. Severe adversity causes us to grow up. We mature in our walk with God. We could say: "I quit! Ministry is not worth this heartache." But why give up on the assignment God has for your life when you know all things work together for good to them that love God and to them who are called according to His purpose? (Romans 8:28)

❧

MAKE ME AND MOLD ME, GOD!

God intends for us to become like Christ (1 John 3:2); holy and without blame (Ephesians 1:4) and to conform to the image of Christ (Romans 8:29). Here are just a <u>few</u> qualities that have grown in me as God molded (and continues to mold) my character.

• Greater appreciation of others (1 Thessalonians 5:18)
• Greater commitment to the things of God (Psalm 37:5)
• Greater compassion for others (1 Peter 3:8)
• Confident (and not ashamed) of the person God made me (Philippians 4:13)
• Contentment at all times (Philippians 4:11)
• Self control (1 Thessalonians 5:22)
• Calmer and a more peaceful heart (John 16:33)
• An ever increasing faith and trust in God (Proverbs 3:5-6)
• A desire to seek God FIRST in EVERYTHING (Matthew 6:33)

I'll never forget when a friend of mine said to me one day, "Saundra, I don't want to go through!" I told her, "I'm going to be very honest with you…I don't want to go through either. Who does?" But the place in which I find myself is disproportionate to the level to which God wants to take me. Therefore, I must go through until God perfects me. I must go through until God says so. None of us are perfect and we are not really all that holy, either. We are always striving for perfection and always pursuing holiness. It is here in that constant state of pursuit that God can develop us, use us, and favor us. But why?

Well, I'm so glad you asked.

QUESTIONS FOR REFLECTION
Are you willing to be persecuted for the name of Christ? Why or Why Not? What are the trials in your life that prove God's power and strength?

THINK ABOUT IT
Name someone in the Bible whom God used but they did not "go through." What does that tell us about our calling to minister?

QUESTIONS FOR DISCUSSION
I listed qualities that have grown in me as God molded my character. What are qualities that have grown in you?

CHAPTER FOUR

❦

Why Must God Deal With Us? What's the Point?

I want to change lanes in this chapter to briefly elaborate on *why* God deals with us. I've told you the **how**—God deals with us through trials—and I've told you the **what**—God develops our character—but I haven't told you the **why.** Why must God deal with us? What is the objective of our trials? If everything has a purpose, what is the purpose of our trials?

There is a point to the pain. When we realize the outcome, it will usher us into a deep gratitude for the process and the trials God brings our way. My desire is that each "purpose" listed will help you to see the benefits (and not just the pain associated with) the trials of life. God wants to:

- *Change us into the image of Christ*
- *Purge away all impurities from our lives*
- *Cleanse us so that we can do his will*
- *Bring forth fruit within us*
- *Prune us so that we can continue to bear fruit*
- *Enlarge our lives*
- *Prepare us for service*
- *Provoke us to seek God in prayer and the Word*
- *Produce spiritual wine in us*
- *Provide us with a new focus and perspective.*

❦

To Change Us Into The Image Of Christ

Throughout the Bible, you will find Scripture after Scripture depicting who Christ is—he is holy, righteous, humble, peaceful, etc. These are the characteristics that God wants to move us toward. Many times, ministers mess up because we concentrate on the short skirts or the baggy pants—and I've done it before. But I've learned to change my perspective. Those external things, while they may be important on the outside, are not as important on the inside of a man. What is most important is that God changes our heart such that we have a desire to be like Christ. Once a person has a desire to change and repent, all of the "stuff" will eventually go away. The key is not to condemn anyone because of how they look. The key is to love everyone so that the love of Christ will transform their lives.

When God deals with us and develops our character, he's developing it so that we can be conformed into the image of His son. There's a scripture that I hold dear to my heart because it was the emphasis verse during my initial sermon. Matthew 5:16 "Let your light so shine that men may see your good works and glorify your father which is in heaven." This is the reason that God needs to change us into the image of Christ; not so that people can see us—because the truth is, I am not all that important. What's really important is that people see the Christ in me. That is the fruit that God is looking for!

ℒ❦

TO PURGE AWAY ALL IMPURITIES

Impurities are everywhere. An impurity could be something as minor as me "embellishing" on my taxes or as major as someone murdering a family member. Regardless of how public our impurity may be, the truth is, God sees them all.

David cried in Psalm 51:7 "Purge me with hyssop, and I shall be clean: wash me, and I shall be whiter than snow." Someone once said to me, "I think I'm going to do my own taxes this year so that I can put in what I want to put in for my deductibles and make that number work out the way I want it to work out." This was a Christian woman who said this to me. She claimed to know Christ. But regardless of her status as preacher or usher, she needed to be purged. Cheating is cheating. This is an impurity, this is scum, and this is waste. God deals with us in order to get that stuff out of us.

TO CLEANSE US SO THAT WE CAN DO HIS WILL

According to Scripture, we must be clean in order to do God's will. James 4:8 reminds us to "Draw nigh to God, and he will draw nigh to you. Cleanse your hands, ye sinners; and purify your hearts, ye double minded." We cannot do the will of God if we are not clean on the inside. Some people say, "I know people who are not where they should be but they are doing God's will." But let me explain that. People may be doing God's work but they aren't necessarily doing God's will. The two are not synonymous. When we do God's work, we join an assembly of people who do good things in the world. A lot of people do the work of the Lord and do not confess Christ as Lord. Just the other day I was watching television as they were showing Duke students rallying together to commemorate the 1-year anniversary of Haiti's earthquake. They were doing God's work. God has called us to love our neighbors. So, anyone can do good works. But, to live out this gospel ministry, good works isn't enough. If they were, good works would get us into heaven. Rather, God has to clean us up so that we can do his will. His will is that we follow his Word, and as we follow his Word, our heart will be changed.

✒

TO BRING FORTH FRUIT

Jesus reminds us in John 15:5 "I am the vine and you are the branches. Those who remain in me, and I in them, will produce much fruit." All of us will bring forth fruit based on the kind of branch we are. If I am the kind of branch who does work for my own glory, then I am going to bring forth fruit that tastes like a person stuck on myself. If I am connected to God the way the Scriptures tell me to be, and everything I do is for God, then the fruit that I bear will have the same love of Christ. It will harmonize with the Word, and not compete against it.

There is no such thing as Saundra's fruit. There is no such thing as a minister's fruit. All fruit belongs to God. And the fruit comes forth because of who God is inside of us. People ask me often, "Can you mentor me?" And I tell them very quickly, "You have to be ready for someone like me to mentor you. I am going to push you toward Christ. I want to make sure you're going to become fruit from the vine of Christ. If that's what you want, then that is what you'll get." I can't just say, "We'll read a book and learn together and talk and go shopping," No! I'm going to push you until you are shaped into the image of Christ.

God wants fruit that will glorify him and ministers that will expand his kingdom.

TO PRUNE US SO THAT WE CAN CONTINUE TO BRING FORTH FRUIT

Pruning involves cutting off dead branches. It also involves cutting off the living branches to improve the shape of a plant and to stimulate growth. In the natural, pruning is essential for fruitfulness. In the next section, I will discuss the root of our secret sins, but if we are going to be fruitful in ministry, God will take us through times of pruning and uprooting. The Amplified Version of John 15:2 states:

He cuts off every branch of mine that doesn't produce fruit, and he prunes the branches that do not bear fruit so they will produce even more.

Pruning is tough and necessary. God has to prune us so that we will continue to be fruitful and have greater fulfillment in Him. God cuts off those things that are dead and He prunes those areas that are producing. Why? Because He is preparing us for an even greater and more effective ministry!

TO ENLARGE OUR LIVES

No doubt about it, God wants to promote us. Scripture reminds us that "promotion doesn't come from the east, nor the west nor the south. Promotion comes from God" (Psalm 75:6-7). God wants to bless us. There are things that God wants us to do in ministry. In order for us to do it, there must be some sort of expansion. It's not about a title, because what God wants to do in you is bigger than a title; it's about enlarging our spiritual lives; taking us to a higher level in Him. This is another reason God allows us to go through. In order to promote us and enlarge our lives, He has to take away things that are not like Him. Sometimes He removes church activities or work activities, or bad habits or tendencies. Either way, in order to enlarge us, God has to deal with us so that we can be prepared for the season to which He is taking us. There are spiritual enlargements, financial enlargements, and social enlargements, but none of this happens without preparation.

✒

TO PREPARE US FOR SERVICE

Preparation is very important. Most ministers would love to avoid it but the truth is, God must prepare us for service. There are some things that only preparation will teach. It is sometimes difficult to endure, but the level of service will determine how much God will have to prepare the vessel (minister), or the depth of preparation for the vessel.

When I first learned this, I found myself in situations that made me wonder, "God, why do you have me in this?" Sometimes the preparation wasn't horrific, it was just a major challenge. For example, I moved from being a professor at the University to the Vice Presidency position in 2001. I remember going to work and saying to God, "I have no idea what I'm doing. I don't know how community colleges operate. How in the world am I going to lead these people? God please help me!" I didn't know what God was preparing me for in July 2001 when I took that job. On top of that, my son was born in September. It was challenging and tax-ing, but at the same time, it was rewarding. Looking back, God was using this position to help me understand how to delegate, communicate, and operate in government and boards. These ten years have taught me so much that I now have incorporated into ministry. So with one promotion that happened ten years ago, God was literally preparing me for international ministry. You couldn't have told me that before. But I know it now, and it has changed the way I see my life today.

❧

TO PROVOKE US TO SEEK GOD IN PRAYER AND THE WORD

Sometimes, as ministers, we may find ourselves spending less time in prayer and in the Word. But devotional time with God is essential to our ministry. This is something that God has called us to do in order to bear fruit. We must continue in prayer and in the Word, and if we're not doing that, then God will deal with us to get us back on that path.

You know some people believe, "When things are good, we don't pray or read the Word. And the only time we seek God, it's because something is wrong." Unfortunately, this is what it takes for some people to get back into the Word like they need to be. The early church was committed to prayer and meditation on a daily basis. In the same way, it is imperative that we seek God in prayer and in the Word, constantly and consistently. Don't make God have to deal with you... just stay in His face!

𝒮♥

TO PRODUCE SPIRITUAL WINE IN US

Scripture reminds us in Luke 5:37, that "no one pours new wine into old wineskins. If he does, the new wine will burst the skins, the wine will run out and the wineskins will be ruined. New wine must be poured into new wineskins." When God wants to do something new in us, it is typically something God wants to develop that is not presently there. Thus, He takes us through a crushing process so that he can produce new wine. God can't pour new wine into us if we are the same way that we used to be. In other words, if we still have waste on the inside of us, then God has to crush it out of us because He can't place new things in us if we are still carnal, old wineskins.

If you think about a wineskin, you know that a new wineskin is very strong. It can hold whatever you pour into it. As wineskins get older, they develop fine holes inside of the wineskin. If God wants to pour something new into us, and we're not spiritually prepared for it, then we may hear it but we will not be able to receive it or contain it. It won't hold. Like old wineskins, it will seep out by the holes. The point is this: there must be a crushing process so that the old wineskin can go away and God can pour new wine in a new wineskin.

TO PROVIDE US WITH A NEW
FOCUS AND PERSPECTIVE

As ministers, many of us don't like change. We want to keep the same focus in ministry. We want to keep the same perspective. I used to have this thing about young men wearing their pants hanging down. I would comment about how it looks and how they couldn't run without their pants falling down. But, one day the Lord showed me that I was looking at the wrong thing. A friend of mine agreed. She said, "We need to stop looking at people from their outward appearance, but instead, see them as God sees them." How can we minister to people if we can't get past what they look like?

Another example of this is my father-in-law, a great pastor and man of God who went home to be with the Lord in 2002. At an appreciation dinner (held in his honor), he stood up to talk about when he had gotten very sick. He said the Lord had to lay him out in order to give him a new focus. While lying there, God showed him that he was actually looking at the wrong thing for many years. When he got off of his sickbed, he made a decision to "focus on the heart." He taught, until the day he died, "the outside will come later, but for now, see the heart." This new perspective allowed his ministry to radically change. He began to look at people differently, and people began to appreciate him more.

When God is ready for us to have a new focus and perspective, He has to take out the old traditions and perspectives. We all have traditions and customs that we've done forever, and that is fine. But make sure you are not missing God. There may be a new group of people that God is calling us to, and we have to understand people and accept a new perspective to do ministry. Maybe God is saying that we must get past our traditions in order to reach certain groups of people.

When I look back on my own life, and I think about the losses I've had—the trials and even physical afflictions that I've had, I won't say that knowing the purpose of these trials made it easier. It didn't. It wasn't easy and I would not want to go through it again. But it did change my perspective in the end. It grew me up. Now that God has developed my character in those areas, I am far more ready to do ministry than I was before. And the more I do ministry, the more he roots out of me.

Are you ready to get to the root?

QUESTIONS FOR REFLECTION

Name a time when God gave you a new perspective on ministry? Was it hard to implement change? How did your new perspective develop your character?

THINK ABOUT IT

The outcomes are far greater than the trials. Which of the above categories have you found to be the most difficult to endure? Why?

QUESTIONS FOR DISCUSSION

As a minister of the gospel, do you feel you are prepared for ministry? How has God prepared you personally? What steps did you have to take to arrive to this place?

Chapter Five

Why Must God Root Out My Secret Sins? Can't Those Stay?

By this point, we have considered several scriptures that give us a better understanding about why ministers must "go through." In summary, we "go through" because God wants to grow us and develop us. We've learned the method (how) and we know the objective (why). But what about those areas in our lives that displease God? What about when God needs to do surgery on those secret sins that nobody sees?

My first exposure to secret sins was at a spiritual encounter in 2003. I had never heard of the term "secret sin," so I had no concept that secret sins resided in my personal life. While I was at this encounter, a session was held called "Root Spirits." Well, needless to say I did not consider myself as someone who had any root spirits – until the facilitator distributed to each of us a sheet of paper. When I read that paper, all I could do was repent for those root spirits that I had let become a part of me. Those root spirits manifested themselves as secret sins! These are sins I would never want to admit to having, but I had to be delivered from. It was at this point in my spiritual life that God literally cut me open and revealed to me how He saw my heart.

As a minister I would never want to admit that I had secret sins. But, repentance and experiencing the freedom of being set free from those secrets within has been one of the most amazing parts of my journey as a minister.

As we prepare to do the work of ministry, ministers will seldom pray these words found in Psalm 19:12b: "Cleanse me from my secret faults." Let's face it: As ministers we do not want to admit that secret faults or secret sins exist within us. The assumption is that ministers don't have secret sins. The assumption by many is that ministers are perfect. But, I'm writing to correct that falsehood right now. According to Romans 3:23, "We all have sinned and come short of the glory of God." If that is the case, then we all also have secret sins that God must constantly root out in order to keep us focused on ministry. Cleansing us from our "secret faults" is one additional reason that ministers may experience trials and tribulations. God takes us through not because He wants to pick on us or play with our emotions. Instead, God wants to prevent us from falling to those secret sins that come in to destroy our focus. God roots out secret sins for our good and for His glory.

❧

SECRET SINS: DEFINED

You may be asking yourself, what are secret sins? Well, secret sins are those inward sins that no one can see. They are invisible to the naked eye but visible and obvious to God. Areas where we struggle the most yet we feel we cannot ask for help, are secret sins. Things we rarely preach about and many ministers fail to admit they exist, are secret sins. We hide them so well – even from ourselves, that we become comfortable operating in ministry, even though secret sin exist within us and have become a part of us.

Secret sins attack our character. They try to stop us from being completely transparent. We say one thing, but internally we hide those emotions and feel opposite than that which we preach. This is the door that leads to our secret faults. Some of these faults may play out in our actions or words, but most of the time, we hide them from the world. Many people think that secret sins are only obvious sins that show up on the outside of us; but there are some secret sins that exist deep within. God needs to root out these sins and purify us from these faults. This is the purpose of rooting it all out.

We try to put on fake smiles so that no one will know what we are feeling. Or we continue to preach and teach on the outside, but inside we know there is a struggle. Bitterness, jealousy, unforgiveness and judging others were some of my secret sins that God had to root out of me. Can you admit, at this point, that there are some secret sins in you?

It is important that you see a list of secret sins. This list, though not exhaustive, will give you clear examples of those sins that we often keep hidden from others.

- *Arrogance*
- *Pride*
- *Haughtiness*
- *Callousness*
- *Self-centeredness*
- *Self-righteousness*
- *Hard heartedness*
- *A bad temper*

- A vengeful spirit
- Lustfulness
- Manipulation and control
- A "know-it-all" attitude
- Judgmental and critical

We do ourselves a grave disservice if we think of secret sins as less serious than the sins everyone sees. Jesus taught in Matthew 5:21-30 that sins concealed from view carry the same guilt as a sin that manifests itself in ungodly behavior. All sin, whether done in public or in secret, is an assault against God. God knows the innermost secrets of our heart. He can clearly see all sin no matter how much we think we are hiding it. Remember, Scriptures tells us: "God sees not as man sees, for man looks at the outward appearance, but the Lord looks at the heart" (1 Samuel 16:7).

The list above describes those secret sins of the mind and heart. These mindsets can produce acts of sinful behavior, but they are in no way lesser than another violation of God's law. For example, if you have a lustful spirit, you are not superior to one who fornicates. If you indulge in lustful thoughts, you are capable of committing fornication. The only difference is, you just haven't acted it out yet. Thus, your secret life is the real test of your character. For the Bible says, "As a man thinks in his heart, so is he" (Proverbs 23:7).

❧

THERE WAS NOTHING SAFE ABOUT MY SECRET SIN

There is nothing safe about harboring a secret sin. If left unchecked, secret sins may stop you from moving forward in ministry. I want to give an example of two personal secret sins that God had to root out of me. I call them the "double J's": *judging* and *jealously.* Although I hate to admit either one of these, I know that my candidness will help others to be free as well.

I have been known to have a judgmental attitude. If people did not do things the way I felt they should be done, I would judge them in my mind and with my mouth. I was both the judge and the jury! Jesus clearly tells us not to judge (Matthew 7:1-5), and I knew it was wrong to judge others. But one day, God showed me just how hypocritical and self-righteous I really was.

One of the leaders in my church made a decision that I didn't agree with. In addition, she said something to me that I felt was hateful and hurtful. I reacted verbally and emotionally. I expressed to my husband how I didn't agree with this lady's decision and I did not like what she said to me. Even further, I started to place a value judgment on the lady because of a decision she made. In effect, I took the situation to an entirely different place, and made a conclusion about who she was in connection to a decision she had made.

Later, the Holy Spirit convicted me. God told me to repent for judging her. Matthew 7:1 kept coming to my mind:—*Judge not that ye be not judged.* It ran through my mind so much that I eventually recognized the point: God was using this verse to deal with my secret sin of judging others. Nobody knew it existed within me (except God and now, my husband), but I had to repent for this action. Thereafter, I decided to make a conscious effort to ask God whenever the situation revisited itself, *"Lord, how do You want me to respond? In what way should I respond so that my words echo the sentiments of Your heart?"*

I often blamed my judgments on the fact that people were not lining themselves up with the Word of God. But was I lined up with the Word myself? Matthew7:2-5 declares,

"For in the same way you judge others, you will be judged, and with the measure you use, it will be measured to you. Why do you look at the speck of sawdust in your brother's eye and pay no attention to the plank in your own eye? How can you say to your brother, 'Let me take the speck out of your eye' when all the time there is a plank in your own eye? You hypocrite, first take the plank out of your own eye, and then you will see clearly to remove the speck from your brother's eye."

That experience helped me to see that my judgmental reaction was a secret sin. Because God exposed the secret sin, I had to acknowledge that it existed within me. When I admitted my struggle to God about judging others, it was difficult. But it was necessary for my spiritual growth. God rooted it out and I am eternally grateful. I now make it an everyday practice not to cast judgment on others. I have learned to shut my mouth and leave him or her in God's hands.

The other part of my "double J" was the secret sin of jealousy. Many people only think jealously occurs when a rivalry exists. But my experience with jealously had to do with what others could do that I could not. When my husband and I were going through the infertility process, I dealt with jealousy. I was jealous of my friends, not because of who they were but because of what they could do. They could get pregnant and I couldn't. I was envious. They had the ability to do something my husband and I could not do. This kind of jealously, (although warranted because I thought I had the right to be jealous), is sin. It is not characteristic of a woman who loves God. I didn't realize it, but basically I was being controlled by my own desires (1 Corinthians 3:3). I was still preaching, teaching and doing ministry, but on the inside, jealously was tearing me apart. Therefore, God had to deal with me and root it out of me. How God rooted out my secret sins goes beyond the scope of this book. However, I have often given my testimony of freedom when I preach and teach! Each time I give my testimony I experience the scripture from Revelations 12:11, "they were overcome by the blood of the lamb and the word of their testimony."

☙

One More Time - Secret Sins Must Be Exposed!

Secret sins must be exposed and rooted out. Often we don't want to admit that they exist when God reveals them to us, but in order to get free from secret sins, we have to first acknowledge that they are there and then be willing to go through the process of having them rooted out.

Many times, when God shows you yourself, (that is, when you see yourself the way God sees you), you are almost always led to ask God to forgive you. Repentance doesn't feel good but it certainly is necessary! In a sense, you feel like you're starting your salvation process all over again, and I've had to do it many times. The good news, however is, it's all for the purpose of God developing our character. Secret sins make us into something that God doesn't want us to be. When secret sins are not taken care of, or when we don't allow God to deal with them, we end up falling frequently because of those sins. Eventually, we become ineffective in ministry. How could I truly help others deal with jealousy when it hadn't been rooted out of me yet? How could I teach effectively on forgiveness when unforgiveness and resentment was lodged deep in my heart against someone? I cannot minister in these areas until God roots out the secret sin and teaches me how to live according to His Word.

Now I am not a preacher who believes that one person can minister in every single area. I believe there are areas that God assigns us to minister to, and God takes us through a series of events for the purpose of helping others in those particular areas. Having said that, the examples I shared have benefited me in two ways. First, it has helped in the development of my character. Second, these experiences have helped to form me spiritually and emotionally. The lessons I have learned through the "rooting out" and the "going through" season was this: neither of these processes were about me. Yes, God developed my character. Yes, He made me stronger and matured me in Him. But these actions were for the purpose of giving Him glory and expanding His kingdom. Don't forget the big picture!

𝓛♥

PRAY FOR UNDERSTANDING!

Whenever God is rooting out those areas that don't belong, we should pray not only about the situation but also for understanding. *What is God trying to develop in us? What is this teaching us?* Most times, when we are in a situation or circumstance, we only pray for God to get us out A.S.A.P.! The better prayer is to ask God, *Why do you have me here?* If I'm in this situation, the next question should not be *Where is the exit sign?;* it should be *What, Lord, do you want me to learn?*

There is a deeper purpose for every experience we encounter. We may not like it or understand it, but our uncertainty about the situation is the very reason we need to pray for understanding. I am a firm believer in Proverbs 4:7 "in all thy getting, get an understanding." The better I understand, the more likely I will be able to recognize when God is developing something in me or rooting something out of me that shouldn't be a part of me because it's not pleasing to Him.

QUESTIONS FOR REFLECTION
What does God desire to root out of you? What are those things that are inside of you that people cannot see?

THINK ABOUT IT
When you find out about someone else's secret sin, what do you do? Judge? Gossip? Pray?

QUESTIONS FOR DISCUSSION
What do you believe God is saying to us by exposing the secret sins of popular ministers and pastors? Is there a lesson to be learned? Is the lesson for us or for them? What is the bigger picture behind this exposure?

CHAPTER SIX

What are the Major Areas that I can expect to be Tested?

Tests are a part of learning. They come with the territory. Most students don't like tests, many teachers don't enjoy designing the test, but the only way to know how far a student has grown, is if she is tested. After every test comes an evaluation. Your evaluation tells the teacher if you are ready for the next level of work or if you need to stay behind another year and learn what you were taught all over again. If a minister is not tested, then she is stagnant. Our tests are God's method of evaluating us. He desires to prepare us, equip us and strengthen us in those areas that need more growth and development. When God tests us, He often tests us in major areas of our lives and minor areas. This chapter will highlight seven major areas where a minister's life must be tested. These areas include:

- *Spiritual Life*
- *Personal/Social Life*
- *Home Life*
- *Educational Life*
- *Ministerial Life*
- *Marital Life*
- *Financial Life*

SPIRITUAL LIFE
You also, like living stones, are being built into a spiritual house to be a holy priesthood, offering spiritual sacrifices acceptable to God through Jesus Christ. (1 Peter 2:5 NIV)

One of my favorite books is called the *Celebration of Discipline: the Path to Spiritual Growth,* by Richard Foster. It's my favorite because it encourages me to constantly move toward spiritual growth. This book taught me how to grow spiritually. It was a blueprint for showing me the things I should be doing not just as a minister, but as a Christian. I love it because although it is primarily used as a seminary text, it is nonetheless an important book that shows us the inward and outward disciplines that all Christians should have.

Your spiritual life is what goes on between you and God. Your spiritual life includes the struggles we experience as well. Now, many people don't believe that Christians struggle, but that is not the truth. Christians struggle internally, and Christians struggle externally. We have to remember that we haven't always been saved. We haven't always lived for Christ. So, there can be areas that we struggle with externally—addictions and habits—and some people don't want to be honest about that, but the truth is, we all struggle. You may have a physical addiction –like sex, or other kinds of internal addictions, like low self-esteem or depression –but our spiritual lives are developed so that God can drive us closer to Him. In our spiritual life, He tests our character such that our spiritual life is more devoted to God. We begin to do those things that God requires of us when He tests our spirit. We pick up spiritual disciplines when we let God work on our spiritual lives.

Ultimately, God wants our spiritual life to be filled with prayer, fasting, reading his Word, and meditating on Him, for the purposes of learning things like simplicity, solitude, submission and service. These are a few things that God wants to develop. Thus, there are times when the internal and external struggles manifest themselves because God wants us to discipline our spiritual life in certain areas. This major test will help us to get closer to God in the long run.

You may be asking, "Saundra, what were your spiritual struggles?" Well I have had many. They often focus around questions that I could not answer or when God responds to something totally different than I expected. Regardless of the context of my spiritual struggles, the outcome was the same. I grew closer to God. I often describe my struggles as God wanting me to learn more of who He is. So the outcome of my struggles is more important than the struggle itself. What have I learned from my spiritual struggles? I have learned about the character that God expects from me and that He will do whatever it takes for me to exhibit His character in my daily life.

❧

PERSONAL/SOCIAL LIFE
But he was wounded for our transgressions, he was bruised for our iniquities: the chastisement of our peace was upon him; and with his stripes we are healed. –Isaiah 53:5

Your social life includes your personal life with friends and family, the way you respond to things that are personal to you, what you do with your free time or where you go on vacation; all of these are areas under the umbrella of "social life." Sometimes, God tests us in our social life because something is impacting or affecting (whether negatively or positively) our character. My example is my brother. People who know "Junior" and me know that my only prayer for him is that he give his life to the Lord. This is a personal struggle for me because I don't want him to die and not know Christ as his personal savior. It's a struggle because I know what I desire for him, but ultimately, the outcome is up to Junior, not me. Every time I think about this personal struggle with my brother, I realize there is nothing I can do but pray even more, and ask God to "open Junior's heart, and allow him to receive You one day." Through this struggle, I have learned that God desires for me to be persistent in my prayers for my brother. I have come to understand how to "pray without ceasing" (1 Thessalonians 5:17).

Another part of my personal life is my mother. All of her siblings have a genetic disease called ataxia. This is a health-related disease where the brain begins to deteriorate after age 50. My mother and all of her siblings have it. Considering the recurrent history in my family, I should have it, too. So, of course, as I approach fifty, the devil begins to play with my mind. He says things like, "Your mother has this disease. Look what it's done to her. Why do you think you're going to be the exception?" He tries to play with my mind so that I enter a place that darkens my perspective. Sometimes I have to snap back into reality and say, "Wait! I am a child of God. I will not allow the enemy to take my mind to a place where I am not supposed to be. I refuse to live in fear of something that will not happen to me. I refuse to believe that this disease will happen to me." Even if symptoms of the disease appear to manifest themselves in small ways during the course of my day, I have learned to immediately declare: "I believe God and by His stripes I am healed." If nothing else, the personal/social tests that God brings your way will drive you to stand on the Word of God.

❧

HOME LIFE
But he that heareth, and doeth not, is like a man that without a foundation built an house upon the earth; against which the stream did beat vehemently, and immediately it fell; and the ruin of that house was great.- Luke 6:39

Home life tests are situations that happen in your home. Your home is your private dwelling. Your home is an intimate place. Most of your fondest memories begin and end in the home. Your home life also takes into consideration your financial life as well. Someone in your home, for example, could've been laid off. Many times, God will test you through this "home life" experience in order to teach you how to depend on Him.

I remember about 5 years ago, we had a sacrificial giving program at our church. We were asked to give above and be-yond our tithes. Now, at the time, our tithe was already a significant amount (in dollar amount) because of the job I had. But, the Lord spoke to my husband and said that we were to double our tithe and sacrifice above and beyond our tithes. When I heard him tell me that, I didn't have a problem doing it because, in my mind, we were financially stable. But soon after, I literally had a life or death experience where I thought I was going to die. Obviously, it wasn't time for me to go home because I am writing this book now, but I came very close to death at that point in my life. Through this experience, I realized that life was short and I went home and decided to do the things that I really wanted to do. I always wanted to be a professor and God set it up that I was able to become a professor at North Carolina State University. But what that also meant at home (speaking of home life) was that I would have to take an extraordinary pay cut. Finances were cut by at least $50,000 a year. Nevertheless, my husband continued to double our tithe and sacrifice in giving at the same amount BEFORE the huge decrease in my pay.

This caused a lot of financial problems. It also caused problems in my home because my husband and I weren't necessarily seeing eye to eye. But my husband is the head of the house, and I was taught to allow him to make certain decisions—especially if those things have to do with the spiritual things of the family—so we continued to give that sacrificial offering on the prior salary we had before I got the new job making less money.

In my mind, it was awful. But God's test taught me a two-fold lesson. First, God taught me that He is in control. He had to build me on the inside, and teach me that if I am obedient to

His word, I would never miss a thing. I literally gave up financial control to my husband. I gave up control and allowed my husband to be the head. I followed him as he followed Christ. And even though I didn't like it, I knew I had to be obedient to God's word and to what my husband believed God was telling him to do. Well, about three years to the day of that financial sacrifice, God blessed me with a job that paid three times as much as my previous job, and God has continued to bless us financially!

Now that I see the big picture, I sometimes think, *What if I would've been disobedient? What if I would've said, "Well Dennis, we're only going to double our tithes based on my professor's salary." What if I would've compromised the original sacrifice?* God was preparing me for the blessing He had in store, three years down the road. This taught me to understand the Scriptures, and respect my husband as the head of the household. As head, it doesn't mean that husbands and wives don't work together (I believe we should), but the most important thing is, our home life should develop things in us that are like God. The home life tests will teach us about intimacy with God and deepen our trust level with Him.

❧

EDUCATIONAL LIFE
But watch thou in all things, endure afflictions, do the work of an evangelist, make full proof of thy ministry.
-2 Timothy 4:5

Sometimes God has to show us that we don't know everything. When God called me to T.E.A.C.H., I had already obtained the Doctorate Degree in Education, but still, God was challenging me to do more. I would engulf myself in study and research. But I realized very quickly that it wasn't enough. So I attended a Christian Writer's Guild Conference, and Jerry Jenkins said something that changed my life. He advised us to fulfill our call and master our craft. He elaborated on 2 Timothy 4:5 – *But watch thou in all things, endure afflictions, do the work of an evangelist, make full proof of thy ministry.*

Basically he was saying, if God has called you to write, then you need to learn and master writing. If God has called you to preach, then you need to learn what it means to preach. I thought about myself. I was running from Divinity School, thinking about my job, my spouse and my child. But God wouldn't allow me to let it go. He was tugging me. I knew there was so much more to be learned about God's word and about teaching and helping others (specifically women) get to that place in God. So I went back to school. I made some sacrifices in my personal life to accommodate for the four years I would spend at Regent University Divinity School. These ended up being the best four years of my adult life.

Constantly, I have thanked God for allowing Jerry Jenkins to speak to a crowd publically and set the course of my educational vocation, without him even knowing it. I will always remember: fulfill your call and master your craft. When God calls us to go out and do the work of a teacher, or an evangelist, that means we have to go and get the skill so that we can do what God has called us to do. The educational tests are intended to show you that God always desires to perfect the gift that He put inside of you, for His glory.

⟋♥

MINISTERIAL LIFE
As every man hath received the gift, even so minister the same one to another, as good stewards of the manifold grace of God.-
1 Peter 4:10

When God calls us to minister, we think everything is going to be a beautiful bed of roses. But let me tell you the truth. When God calls you to minister, He redevelops that which had already been developed. When your ministerial life comes into full swing, you have to prepare in a different way than you did before. Once you answer the call to ministry, all the trials that go along with ministry, will manifest. We think God will take care of everything, and He will, but don't forget: when God is taking care of things for us, He's also responsible for the maintenance. He's building His character within us, He's tearing out things that don't need to be there, and He's laying solid foundation within us so that we won't be tossed to and fro by every wind of doctrine. Why? Because our ministerial life is all about serving others. Whatever He needs to develop in us for others, we have to let Him do that.

Very early in my ministerial life, I had a very good friend of mine let me down. I told her with great excitement, "God called me into the ministry!" I expected her to be excited. I knew she would support me through it all. But to my surprise, she cut me off like a string inside a pair of scissors. She stopped speaking with me. She stopped calling me. I felt forsaken. I would ask, "God, why would she cut me off? What did I do wrong?" In retrospect, I remember telling her about what God was doing in my life and how silent she would become on the other end of the phone. I would be bursting with joy, and she wouldn't say a mumbling word. I could sense something on the phone but I could not identify it immediately. Well shortly after, she literally cut me off. She wouldn't answer my calls for anything and this continued for years. Truth is, she wasn't ready to be where God was taking me, but glory to God, God has brought us back together.

I say this to say: these are the kinds of things that God has to prepare us for. Ministerial tests may come to develop you until you learn contentment, or so you can seek only Him, pursuing only holiness and righteousness in Him. But whatever the reason, God takes us through so that we can better understand submission in our ministerial lives.

We have to serve simply and faithfully. Ministry is a life of service; it's a lifestyle. Ministerial life has nothing to do with externals. I remember this lady told me once, "I can't wait to get my license so I can wear suits like yours." I literally responded, "Well you can go buy the suit any time you want to. You don't need a license to wear the suit." I even gave her the card for the lady I get my suits from. She was caught up in the glamour. I was caught up in God. The lesson in this: Ministry is not about what you wear. At the core, it's about service. If you don't have the character to serve but you say God has called you into the ministry, God will, by any means necessary, do what it takes to develop true service on the inside of you. God will not run the risk of ministers damaging someone else because we don't have true servitude in our hearts. The ministerial life tests will reveal who your real friends are, and God will use this to deepen your walk with Him.

MARITAL LIFE

There is difference also between a wife and a virgin. The unmarried woman careth for the things of the Lord, that she may be holy both in body and in spirit: but she that is married careth for the things of the world, how she may please her husband.- 1 Corinthians 7:34

For those of us who are married or looking to be married, there are a few things you must know if you plan to be both married and in ministry. So often, I see women in ministry but their husbands are not. Women begin to focus and nurture and do the things that we do—and when God calls us to minister, we want to spend all of our time in church, or in the Word, or doing "ministry." But let me be real with you for a moment: if we are going to minister effectively, then God has to first develop your character with your husband. Your first ministry is your home. Your husband is first and your children as well (if you have any). If your family/marital life is not right, then nothing else is going to be right. I love spending time with God and the church, but at times, I need to break away from everything to just spend time with Dennis, my husband. Some days, I'll say, "You have my complete attention. I'm turning my cell phone off and spending quality time just with you."

No questions asked, you must take time to be with your husband. Take the time to develop your marriage. When I began to realize that my husband was going in a different direction from me—He wasn't moving away from Christ at all, but I was changing because I was spending so much time doing church work –I repented and changed. As it stands today, you cannot pay me not to cultivate my marriage daily. It could be as simple as going to Starbucks to get him a cup of coffee or making sure he has a gift card to get his coffee in the morning. Sometimes as women, we have to remember that we are ministers, but at the same time, we are wives. Those things need to be merged. For me, this test wasn't passed overnight. God took me through years of testing and training in order to develop this principal in me. The marital life tests will help you to obtain balance, set priorities, and show your love for God by your ability to love and be present with others.

FINANCIAL LIFE
"Everything in the heavens and earth is yours, O Lord, and this is your kingdom. We adore you as being in control of everything. Riches and honor come from you alone, and you are the Ruler of all mankind; your hand controls power and might and it is at your discretion that men are made great and given strength" -1 Chronicles 29-11-12

I've already written a little about this area in the home life section, but finances are such a major test, they deserve double mentioning. Many times, God sends financial tests our way because we don't want to release everything to Him. Everything includes our money! The above scripture reminds us "everything in the heavens and earth is yours, O Lord, and this is your kingdom." Everything means everything. That means, if we snatch our money back and prioritize money over and above God, then we're not giving God maximum glory. I've learned through so many examples how our finances are His and I've learned to be good stewards over what God has given to me. I truly believe we endured the financial turmoil because God knew that He would place me in a ministry and, later, place me in charge of finances. Now I understand what to do with a budget, how to be in charge of a budget, and how to manage, allocate, and organize financial records. This had to be developed through my financial life.

Trust me, God tests us because He has something greater in store for us. He wants us to learn to be good stewards over what He has given. Many times I've heard people say, "I'm going through! I wish God would bless me financially," but contrary to popular belief, I've learned that the best financial blessing is not having money. When you have fewer dollars, you tend to have greater faith. You begin to see God more clearly. You become a better steward over what God entrusts you with. Financial tests are meant to humble us, and teach us dependency on God. When you pass this test, your faith has been increased.

Spiritual Life, Social Life, Home Life, Educational Life, Ministerial Life, Marital Life, and Financial Life. These are all the major areas where our character must be tested. Some of them are easier to endure than others, but ultimately, every minister must go through a series of major tests in our lives.

But Saundra, what about the minor tests? Well, I'm so glad you asked.

QUESTIONS FOR REFLECTION
Of the major tests mentioned above, which tests have you passed? Which have you failed? How do you know you passed or failed? What did you learn?

THINK ABOUT IT
If God gave you an examination on the seven areas above, what would your grade assessment be? Rate yourself on each major test. Give yourself an A, B, C, D or F.

QUESTIONS FOR DISCUSSION
Which area have you found most difficult to pass? Why is it so difficult? What are your frustrations? How is God using this to further develop your character?

CHAPTER SEVEN

♑

What are the Minor Areas that I can expect to be Tested in?

In the Old Testament, there were both Major Prophets and Minor Prophets. The Minor Prophets were just as important as the major ones. The only difference is, the Major Prophets were designated for the longer books. Minor Prophets represented the shorter books. The same is true for this chapter. When I use the term minor tests, I do not mean to suggest that some tests are less significant than others. The word "minor" simply identifies a subcategory under the major tests we've discussed in the previous chapter. By now, we have reviewed the subject of tests in general, but now, I need to discuss this subject with more specificity.

It is my hope that, after you read this chapter, you will walk away better prepared for the big tests, the little tests, and the middle-sized tests. Each test you endure is important; for it will equip you and prepare you for the ministry within.

Let's focus on some specific tests. Some of these tests have been gleaned from other resources, like Frank Damazio's *The Making of a Leader* and Joyce Meyers' *A Leader in the Making*. Others, I have coined myself as a "Saundra-ism." But the majority of these tests, I have personally experienced.

In *Making of a Leader*, Frank Damazio describes spiritual tests as essential for ministry preparation. He believes that God intentionally places ministry leaders in desperate situations so that the people who don't feel the true call to ministry can have the freedom to drop out during the preliminary stages. If you make it through these tests, then you are truly called for ministry. The point he is trying to make is simple yet profound: ministers must be divinely appointed by God. Ministry is not an optional vocation; it is a divine assignment. Damazio's philosophy is true. God will test his leaders to equip them with the spiritual understanding necessary to guide His people. The outcome of passing these tests will benefit the shepherd inwardly, and it will edify the sheep outwardly.

20 Minor Tests

1-Time Test

The purpose of the time test is to help us learn patience. Time tests force us to trust God. When we first get called into ministry, we want to move quickly. But God may be saying, "Wait a minute. I have a different task for you." Then, He takes us through the time test. God takes us through this to show us that "the ministry I called you to is not yours." We must do things God's way (not our way). We must do things in God's own time (not our time).

Here is an example from the Word of God. In Genesis (chapters 12-18), God promised Abraham a nation. He said his descendants would be more than the grains of sand. But this promise didn't happen in Abraham's time. God did this in His own time so that He could show Abraham and his wife, Sarah, that He was in control. Abraham even tried to do his own thing with his concubine, Hagar. But it wasn't until Abraham said to God, "You're in control" that God came in and gave Sarah a son like He had promised. In order for Abraham to see God's promise fulfilled in terms of his descendants, he could not do it in his own way. This is how God gave him the time test.

✍❧

2-WORD TEST

The purpose of the Word test is to help us depend on God until His word comes to pass. Oftentimes, we must reject our own resources and depend only on God. There may be times when you have studied for an exam, and you've received all the right counsel—you've done everything that you know to do, and still, things are happening to you. Most of the time, God is using these situations to prove Himself in and by His word. Ministers must learn: it is not what we can do with our own resources. Yes, God gives them to us, but we cannot depend on them for our resolution. We must depend on God's Word.

Joseph is my biblical example for this test. In Genesis 37-45, we discover that Joseph's brothers were jealous of him; so jealous, they sold him off to slavery. Joseph became number two to Pharaoh in Egypt. Then he was falsely accused by Potiphar's wife, and was imprisoned. So Joseph had to learn the lesson that God is teaching us through the Word test. His resources were not going to move him from where he was to where God would have him to be. He had to depend on God. When he was in prison, he interpreted the dreams of the butler and the baker, but both of them forgot him. This teaches me that we cannot depend on man as our resource. We have to depend on God. God needed Joseph to stay there a little longer in order to teach Him some things. God needed to develop his character.

The Word Test helps us to know, without a shadow of doubt, that God's word is true. When we experience the Word coming to pass in our lives, then the Word will become alive in our ministry.

☙

3 – CHARACTER TEST

The Character test will teach you to stand on the Word of God in the midst of temptation. This test will manifest in our lives when we find ourselves surrounded by those things that are not like God. We have to decide, "Am I going to do what I know will be pleasing to God or am I going to fall for this sin?" These tests do not typically happen in front of people. Our character is tested in private, and proven in public. But let me be clear: God does not tempt us to sin (James 1:13). God isn't that kind of God. God may allow us to be placed in a situation where temptation is present, but the key is, we have to make the decision. These are the qualifications of a character test. They are not tests that people will know you have encountered. They are not tests that people will gossip about if you fail. Rather they are tests that will show you how capable you are to stand firmly in the Word of God (or not).

Example: An old beau shows up in your life and you're married. They start talking to you by email. Next thing you know, you're on the phone. Then, you want to see them, and it builds and builds and builds. You know it's wrong. You know it is something God is not pleased with. And now you're at a point that you have to choose: *do I give into temptation or do I decide to be true to God and to my spouse?* Your character is an integral part of your ministry. The choices you make determine the level of effectiveness you have over those God has assigned you to. Let your character be true: both in the spotlight and behind-the-scenes.

4-MOTIVATION TEST

The Motivation test will teach you to make God your sole motivation. When God is calling you into ministry, there will be times that you are excited and thrilled. And then there will be times when you have no motivation at all. You'll look around and soon recognize that certain people don't motivate you. You'll look within and realize you can't even motivate yourself. And then, you begin to wonder, "God did you *really* call me to this? Please send someone to motivate me!"

The key is that you have to choose God. God gives us the motivation/drive to do what He has called you to do. People may not know the purpose behind your calling. That's why our motivation has to come from God. It cannot come from external forces, for they may only show up when things are good. Let me be honest with you: The motivation test is a hurtful reality. God begins to show you how people are looking at you. He even reveals what people are saying about you. But the good news is, it only drives you closer to God. You cannot depend on anybody but God.

I've found that God will continue to test you in this motivation area until He gets you to the point that you know God is always with you, God has always called you, and your motivation and decisions are based on him, and not man.

✒

5-SERVANT TEST

The servant test will train you into doing what God has called you to do, even when it isn't what you want to do. We talk about this test a lot, but when we are asked to live it out, it becomes a different situation. Sometimes in ministry, we think to ourselves "Why would they ask me to do something like this?" We claim "ministry rights" over some things, but we remove our name from the list of other things—usually the stuff that we don't enjoy doing. What we don't realize is—the areas we don't like just may be the places where God is requiring us to be on task. God calls us to carry out whatever He assigns—whether it is to write a book, preach a sermon, work with homeless people, teach children, etc. Servants of God are to do what God says do, no matter how menial a task we think it is.

Here's an example. Because of the job I have and the positions I've been given in church, people sometimes react strongly when they catch me in the back working with the children. I've even heard people say, "Saundra, you're an elder. You minister to so many, you teach to hundreds. How can you go back there and work with children?" My response is simple. I say to them, "Well, God called me to be a mother of a 9 year old son, and that means I must take time with him as well as the other children at my church as well." For 6 years I worked in the children's ministry. It was not my favorite assignment all the time, but it was my assignment nonetheless. I sat there with them, gave out snacks, I washed dishes—I'm learning what it means to be a servant of God in all areas of my life. The same is true for my household ministry. Sometimes, my husband will ask me to do things for him as his wife and some people may say, "Doesn't your husband know how busy you are?" But they don't understand the servant's test. No matter how busy I think I am, God teaches us how to put things into proper perspective. I am never too busy to serve my husband. As a woman of God and as a minister of the Gospel, we are called to serve in various areas. But nothing is a menial task when God calls us to it. Be careful not to become so high and mighty in your calling that you forget to serve.

✍❧

6-WILDERNESS TEST

The wilderness test is your opportunity to see God clearer than ever before. Usually, before you embark upon this test, you feel spiritually dry. God may take you through a season where you feel nothing. You feel like there is no fruit in what God is calling you to do. You may even feel barren. You find yourself saying, "I don't feel or hear you, God."

People see the wilderness as a terrible place to be in. But the wilderness is a gift if you endure the test. In the wilderness is where we learn to push toward God more and more. During this test, you learn the value of time. Ann Graham Lotz (Billy Graham's daughter) once said, "Don't waste your wilderness time." Don't sit there and sulk, saying woe is me! Ask yourself, *What am I going to do while I'm in it?" What is God trying to teach me?* This is where you throw yourself in the word of God and prayer. Take advantage of it. All He wants us to do is to seek Him.

My wilderness experience occurred during my first year of T.E.A.C.H. I didn't know what to do. I didn't want to study and I couldn't seem to hear from God. I literally said to God, "These women are depending on me for a Word and I'm not hearing from you!" I was dry. I was too embarrassed to let people know that I was in this place. So embarrassed, I would not reach out for help. *I'll just read different books,* I thought. But nothing happened. I was in this wilderness because so many things had taken priority over God. I had allowed the work of ministry and business to come before my relationship with God. I was doing more for the "ministry" than I was spending time with the One who placed the ministry in me. After much wasted time, I realized that all God wanted me to do was dive into His word like never before. When I began to do that, I began to experience Matthew 6:33 in a new way and it became my life scripture!

✒

7-MISUNDERSTANDING TEST

It happened to Jesus all of the time in the Gospel. He was misunderstood. When people can't receive because they do not understand you, they will reject you. Now, the motivation test will help you to get through the misunderstanding test (if you pass it). People may reject you for different reasons. It could be because you're simply being you, or they are bothered by what you're teaching; or they may have known you *before* He called you and they don't believe the woman you were yesterday should be in ministry today.

Whatever the reason, being misunderstood isn't a bad thing. It's actually a blessing. When people reject you, this is how you know without a shadow of a doubt that God is calling you. When you are rejected, you have to be prepared to depend on God – even if you have to walk by yourself. Christ had to do it. He endured being misunderstood so that He could focus on being the Savior, the healer, the teacher, and the deliverer. He continued to do what the Father called Him to do. In the same manner, you must continue with God even if you have to be by yourself. Even if people are sleeping through it (Jesus' disciples were asleep and He had to go by himself), you must make up your mind, move on and follow God.

❤

8-PATIENCE TEST

You may wonder what the difference is between the patience test and the time test. The time test will *try* your patience and help you to realize that God isn't doing it the way you thought He would. But the patience test will *build* and *develop* your patience until you finally say, "I surrender Lord. I trust that it will all happen in Your timing and on your schedule."

Trust me. The patience test is coming to see how much we're listening. God allows this test to occur to make sure we are adhering to His orders and not our own. The calling will be fulfilled on God's schedule. The project will be completed when God says "it is finished." You just have to develop patience so that God will see your determination to trust Him until the promise is fulfilled.

℘

9-FRUSTRATION TEST

The frustration test is what we experience when we feel our life and ministry goals are unachievable. Many women talk to me about what God is calling them to do, but for whatever reason, it just doesn't happen. They often express with great frustration, "I know God has called me to start this ministry," but when they open their eyes, they find themselves not living it out.

A ministry associate of mine was called to work with women who had cancer. She herself had both breasts removed as a result of cancer. She felt like God called her to help women see beauty in themselves even through this disease. As she began to move toward what God had called her to do, her personal life began to spiral. Her marriage and her relationship with her children were attacked. She wondered, "God, why in the world are you calling me to do this and all these things are happening to me?" She finally said, "I understand why I had to go through this period of frustration. Everything I went through in my marriage and with my children was so that other women could learn how to go through life with cancer. I needed to understand all aspects of life, living with cancer."

I looked at her and asked, "What do you mean by that?" She went on to say, "Having cancer doesn't mean everything else just stops. Cancer is just one thing. Life still happens around it. I still went through in my marriage. I still had to endure my daughter getting pregnant in college. But God showed me, in the midst of this disease, how to move forward through my frustration. Women still needed to be ministered to. And I couldn't let life dictate ministry. I had to persevere."

The same lesson she taught me, I desire to relay to you. I know you may be frustrated. But in the midst of it all, continue to move forward. Dive headfirst into His word. God is using this frustration to teach you something.

❧

10-WARFARE TEST

The Warfare Test will require you to call people in to pray and intercede. While going through this test, you will experience spiritual opposition. Our warfare is spiritual. The enemy will try to stop you. You can't be in spiritual warfare and try to fight it with the things of this world. Ephesians 6:10-18 tells us what to do. We are facing spiritual opposition. You have to remember: there is a spiritual opponent trying to oppose your desire to expand God's kingdom. The enemy does not want that call to move forward because he does not want the kingdom to expand. As we go through, we will have to help others through their personal warfare as well. Put on your armor, and use the weaponry God has given you to defeat and conquer every scheme the enemy tries to throw your away.

When we begin to deepen our relationship with God, our passion will intensify. I've noticed that every time my passion intensifies, the devil attacks me even more. But God's word reminds me that the enemy is defeated. In the end, God will win the war! Keep that in mind. The devil will try to take you in, but he will fail. It is not our battle to fight. It is spiritual opposition. This battle belongs to the Lord. It's already won.

✍❦

11-SELF-WILL TEST

The self-will test is your garden of Gethsemane experience. In the garden is where we hear Jesus say, "not my will but thy will be done." In other words, it is no longer about Him--but God. The human flesh says, "I really don't want this." But the Spirit says, "I have to go through with this. I have no other choice." God turns our desires. You have passed this test when you can say, "I really want to be doing something else, but I will do what you want me to do, Lord."

We must understand that the plans we have, whether for ministry, personal or professional reasons –are our plans. When

God takes us through the Self-Will Test, we realize how many things we never sought God about, as it relates to our plans. We exchange our will for God's will, and we deny ourselves so that God might get the glory out of our lives.

With T.E.A.C.H., I only wanted to work with women in ministry and leadership. My focal point was women who were already working in ministry through leadership roles. But, God began to show me the personal and spiritual issues of women. Women –all women—needed to be taught. All women needed to be healed. As a result, my heart began to break for these women. God reminded me that T.E.A.C.H. belonged to Him. My Self-will had to be broken. I kept trying to do things for the women that were in ministry but I was never at ease and peace until God broke my will. The ministry had to do what God wanted it to do. When I realized that, I surrendered the ministry back into God's hands. Indeed, it was never about my will within this ministry, it was always about God's!

❧

12 - USAGE TEST

The Usage Test will teach you how to cultivate your gift when there is no demand for it. Often times, ministers church-hop in hopes of finding their opportunity to exercise their God given ministry. Whether you are being used before the people (preaching, teaching) or behind them (cleaning the church), you must learn to be content. You may be asking, "Why hasn't the leadership in my local church asked me to pray or do anything before the people?" The answer is: it isn't your time yet. God is making sure that your ministry is not all about what you want but all about what He needs. If you are used too quickly, you can get a mindset that you (in your own strength) have the answers that people are desperate for. That's a mistake.

I heard a pastor talking about a young man in his church. The pastor was assigning him work that the young man believed was beneath his calling. He wanted to preach, but the pastor knew he wasn't prepared. The young man left the church and havoc broke out. He wasn't mature enough for the call of duty as a minister. The call to minister is not synonymous with the term "preach to the nations." You shouldn't need to be asked to serve; being licensed is an invitation to do what needs to be done. Serve the kids. Clean the bathrooms. Let people see there's more to ministry than teaching. If you truly want to be used by God, the only immediate thing you should be doing is serving.

✥

13 - PROMOTION TEST

When you are in ministry but find yourself not moving the way you expected, you are experiencing the Promotion Test. Many people want to move up in ministry but are simply not ready. The first test to promotion is humility. Before you can be promoted, you must be trustworthy. It is imperative that you know, God is the one who brings promotion--not man and not yourself. Within any ministry, the pastor should remain discerning about your worthiness to be promoted. The pastor knows who is ready for promotion. The question is .....can you be trusted with promotion?

About 7 years ago, there were no elders in my church. There were only "leaders" and I was one of them. My pastor decided to ordain elders in the church. So, several other leaders and I went through training. Right before he told us who the elders would be, he said, "If your name is not on this list, it is because there is something in your life that does not make you worthy of promotion at this time." The list was disseminated and my name was not on it. I was blown away. I had no idea what I had done wrong. After prayer and wise counsel, I wrote my pastor an email because I wanted to correct whatever made me unworthy of becoming an elder. It turned out that a mistake had been made. I was one of four who had been promoted but weren't on the list. My pastor told me that he was excited to see that promotion was not our priority. The four who mistakenly didn't make the list were not concerned with obtaining the title of "elder," we only wanted to know what was displeasing to God. Humility is essential for promotion.

14- STRESS TEST

This test is about learning to trust God, even when you don't understand His ways. "Tis so Sweet" has grown to become one of my favorite hymns. This hymn helped me to trust God more. When there's something I don't understand, I put my confidence in Him. You know, it is hard to be a minister sometimes. A minister has to trust God in the middle of a crisis and you never know the purpose of the stressful time. People expect for us to have all the answers but we have to be content with not understanding; it is only then that we can learn to trust. I don't know why God has allowed the things that I have been through, but all I need to know is that those things were necessary. I can help others learn about trust when they see that I am still living, only because I learned to trust in God.

When my husband and I had twins, and they died, I couldn't understand why God allowed it to happen. I needed answers. My first reaction was to blame God. I was in that hospital, accompanied by my Pastor, when the doctors came to me and said, "I'm sorry, but your babies are gone." Immediately, I turned to him and asked, "Pastor, why did God do this to me?" He calmly said, "You've just got to learn to trust God." I said to him, "No, YOU have to trust him! I want answers!" The truth is, I still don't have an answer. I wanted God to give me a reason. Everything has to happen for a reason. God showed me that you cannot teach reason, you must teach trust. Stress will come. You may not ever know the reason, but when you learn to have confidence in God, you learn how to be totally dependent. I may not like what is happening right now, that my children didn't live, or that as a result, I could not bear children. When I look at where I am, I know that I would not be able to effectively teach others if I didn't go through my own personal stress tests.

☙

15 - SECURITY TEST

The Security Test teaches you to totally depend on God. Despite what you have heard, trusting is a process. I've learned through my personal experiences and by observing the lives of others that the only thing that propels us forward in ministry is learning how to rely on God. When you depend of Him, your heart changes. You no longer depend on men to do anything for you. In Romans 8:28 we learn that everything works together for good for those who love the Lord. That scripture gives me a security that if I do my part, God will do His. Through it all, I have learned to trust, depend and be secure in God alone.

I once heard a testimony of a young woman. She was secure in her job but felt she deserved to be promoted. She wanted more out of life, but she held on to her job as a crutch. After she finally got rid of her security blanket and was willing to give up that job, she was able to solely rely on God. Now she was ready for promotion. Once she shifted her dependency to God, He literally promoted her on the job the next day! Our dependency is never to man. God is the only one who can provide security.

C♥

16 - REJECTION TEST

Rejection is perhaps the most difficult one. This is where you feel like people have rejected you. Your ability to maintain a positive perspective is vital in this test. You know you have passed this test if you continue to move forward in your assignment even though people have refused you. If you don't pass it, you internalize your feelings and you pull yourself down. In the event you fail this test, you will most likely encounter it again, until you master it.

I have been rejected by people whom I have called my friends. I've even wondered if these people were ever my friends to begin with. I thought that when God called you to do a work, everyone would embrace you. I did not understand when they did not. Sometimes I lost the vigor in serving and teaching. I was forced to remember that people rejected Jesus, too. Why was I any better that they wouldn't reject me? The Rejection Test will certainly come. Whether it is ministerial, occupational, or personal, there will be rejection. When you have mastered the Security Test, you will pass the Rejection Test with flying colors.

✐♥

17 - JUDAS' KISS TEST

We all know Judas. He betrayed Jesus. The Judas' Kiss Test is revealed when you are betrayed by your friends. For most, this is the one that hurts the worst, emotionally. You may lose friends. When the devil wants to bring you down, he often works through people, especially people that you consider close to you. Then you realize, they are gone. Judas walked beside Jesus as a disciple. He was bribed to identify Jesus to the chief priests. He kissed Jesus and Jesus was arrested. Jesus knew what Judas was going to do and loved him in spite of his plans.

Being betrayed by friends is not something I tell people to expect. I don't want people to walk around in speculation, wait-

| 80 |

ing for their friends to betray them. All I tell them is that ministry is attractive. There will be people who will get close to you so that they can identify and betray you. If you can love them in spite of their shortcomings and in spite of the hurt in your heart, you have successfully passed this test.

❧

18 - FORGIVENESS TEST

Can you forgive? The Forgiveness Test is another hard one to endure. When you realize that others have done you wrong, you must learn how to forgive them. When we do not allow forgiveness to abound, we leave the door wide open for other sins to enter. If we don't forgive, it can turn into bitterness, which can easily turn into hatred. Many people suffer from infirmities that are rooted in the lack of forgiveness. We can walk around looking holy, but inside, we are killing our heart because we have not forgiven. The Bible says to forgive those who hurt you, and to love those who despitefully use you (Matthew 5:44). We have to continue to do that, even in the midst of our hurt.

My mother-in-law, for example, had to forgive the people in church who had hurt her. Many folks hurt her husband (who was the pastor of their church). It affected her husband so much that his blood pressure shot up and he had a massive heart attack and passed away. I saw how my mother-in-law had to forgive the very people who had hurt her husband. That was hard, but I saw her struggle, work and pray for the strength to forgive. Forgiveness is necessary. You must pass the forgiveness test. You cannot fail. Jesus forgave us when He knew that we were going to persecute him. I don't have a choice.

☙

19 - LOVING THE UNLOVING TEST

This test is about loving the people who irritate you. You don't want to admit that people irritate you, but let's keep it real. Some people get on our nerves! The bible says we have to love everyone just as Christ loved us. God is really teaching you to be patient with people. When we fail to love the unloving, we block the ministry that God has for us. You have to be willing to see them the way God sees you.

Change your perspective.

Stop seeing them as irritating. See them as an opportunity. Ask God to reveal why He has them in your life, and what purpose you will serve in theirs. Remember, everything happens for a reason. There must be a reason God placed that person in your path. God is teaching you that even as wonderful as you are now, you were once unlovable yourself. You may not recognize yourself as unloving until you have to fight to love someone else.

☙

20 - ALONE TEST

This test will make or break a great minister. A minister can't be everybody's buddy. Being alone is something that, as a minister, you're going to have to learn to deal with. You can't be in the presence of God and everyone else too. When I'm not spending time with God, I need to be spending time with my family. Some-times people don't understand that you want to spend time with God. They won't understand that you NEED to be alone with God.

Even if you feel like you're alone, you have to know that God is there. The bible says that He will neither leave you nor for-sake you. He is with you at all times. When you sit in His presence, you can hear him speak. You need the time just to hear. You get that when you can be alone with God, then He will reveal to you, teach you, and speak to you. When you pass the Alone Test, you can minister His word regardless of the setting. It's easy to pass on what you have heard a person say in stillness. Passing this test is vital to spiritual growth.

We must endure and experience these tests as ministers of the gospel. Don't panic though! You were not called because God expects you to pass every test in your own strength. If noth-ing more, these tests teach us how much we need to depend on God. Ministers aren't perfect. We are striving toward perfection. But as we strive, we must remember the essential ingredients of ministry. We can't get caught up in the externals. If we are going to do ministry well, we need to remember the power of the Cross; for only the cross will help us to center ourselves if we are unable to pass these major and minor tests. Hence, the next chapter!

QUESTIONS FOR REFLECTION
Of the minor tests mentioned above, name three tests you've actually passed. What were your experiences like? How have you seen growth in your personal life and public ministry?

THINK ABOUT IT
If you knew in the beginning that God would test you in all of these areas, would you have still said "yes" to the call of ministry on your life? Why or why not?

QUESTIONS FOR DISCUSSION
Who do you most compare to in the Scriptures? How do their tests and your tests relate? Have you experienced a test that was not listed in this chapter? If so, what was it? How did it improve you?

Chapter Eight

✍

The Power of the Cross

Do you remember the hymn, "Old Rugged Cross?" When I was younger, my church usually sang it on Easter Sunday. I heard this hymn countless times and yet, I never really knew what it meant. I sang it and I knew it was about Jesus and the cross that He carried, was nailed to, and eventually died on. But as a child, I never actually understood what *transpired* at the cross. The cross never meant anything to me. I saw it as a piece of decoration in the church. At that time, I was not living a life for God, so of course, I did not fully understand the victory I have today because of the CROSS.

Ministers, beware. There is so much learning to do, and so many things that God may call you to learn, but if you are not enlightened by the fundamentals of your faith—namely, the death, burial, and resurrection of Jesus Christ—then you might as well not preach at all. The power of our ministry is undergirded by the strength of the cross. The anointing that lies within us was activated at the cross. All power has been given to us because of what Jesus suffered through, survived, and conquered over two thousand years ago!

This chapter is more essential than any other. It serves as a reminder to those like me, who tried to understand the cross with our MINDS. Ministers, God wants us to experience the cross with our HEARTS! As preachers and teachers of the gospel, we should renew our understanding of the cross on a consistent basis. Never let the subject of Christ's suffering go stale. There is no way to talk about ministry and not discuss the power of the cross. If we do not begin to concentrate on this subject, our preaching and labor will be in vain.

In this chapter, we will consider two components. First, we will discuss the power of the cross. *What exactly happened to Jesus from a medical perspective? How does knowing this change our perception about the all too familiar story of Crucifixion?* Then, we will discuss the magnitude of the power of the cross for the ministry call on our lives. In this section, we will ask ourselves: *Have I experienced the power of the cross in my life? Have I ever considered its impact on the ministry within?* And, finally: *Lord is it I?*

ℒ♥

THE POWER OF THE CROSS

The first time I taught on the power of the cross, it was in 2011— the same year this book was published. I used to wonder why God wouldn't allow me to finish a book that was 75% complete in 2005! But, what God showed me as I prepared to teach on the cross, was that I did not understand this power at all. I understood it with my head, but God had to ensure I understood the power of the cross with my heart. Permit me to take you into the classroom that day. I opened up by telling the women I was teaching a little about my story:

I (Saundra) was doing what I was bad enough to do. I was proud that I was not getting caught in what my mom called 'sin'. I knew it was sin, but I was enjoying what I was doing and I saw no reason to stop. But then... all hell broke loose in my life. And one Sunday, just like all of you, I gave my life to the Lord. I was told how much He loved me. I was told that Christ loved me so much that He died on the cross for my sins. But no one told me the importance of what Jesus accomplished by His death on the cross. Even after I was saved, I had heard the story so much that I did not even realize what actually took place.

I was trying to understand it with my mind. But what God wanted from me was to experience the cross with my heart. You see, when I experienced the cross with my heart, all those things that had me bound, all the battles that were going on inside of my mind – I was delivered from. I experienced a deliverance and freedom that, to this day, I cannot explain. I can only say that each individual has to experience it for herself.

This morning ladies, God wants you to experience the power of the cross. His desire is not that you understand every detail, but His ultimate desire is that you experience His love! He wants you to radically turn from all known sin in your life. He wants you to receive forgiveness for every wrongdoing you have ever committed. He wants the chains that have bound you to be broken. You can receive that this morning. Once you experience the power of the cross, you will have a freedom that others will not understand.

Let me tell you the story as it is written in the Gospel of Mark 15th chapter. You might say – Saundra I already know the story of the Jesus on the cross. If you were like me, you heard this story as something that happened 2000 years ago. Now you are going to hear the story as though you are a major character; a major player in what is going on.

As you read the following I want you to read as though YOU are there and you are a part of what you are about to read.

Let me warn you, it will not be pretty!

In the 14th chapter of Mark, so many things happened to our Lord and Savior. Jesus prayed His agonizing prayer in the garden of Gethsemane (Mark 14:32-42). Judas betrayed Jesus and Jesus was arrested in the garden (Mark 14:43-50). Jesus was beaten and mocked at Caiaphas' house (Mark 14:65). Peter denied Jesus (Mark 14:66-72). Mark continues to tell us about the events leading to up to the cross in chapter 15.

In Mark 15:1 we are told the enemies of Jesus bound Him and sent Him to Pilate . . .

"Immediately, in the morning, the chief priests held a consultation with the elders and scribes and the whole council; and they bound Jesus, led Him away and delivered Him to Pilate."

Jesus was lashed with a whip, beaten, and mocked by Roman soldiers (Mark 15:15-20).

I do not know about you, but right now, my heart is feeling heavy. I am starting to feel sorry for Jesus. I started asking God some questions. But if I am honest, I did not like the answers I received.

Now I am going to give you specific instructions (that's the teacher in me). Read the following component aloud and say your name where it says to "insert your name." I pray that the impact here will be as emotional and spiritual for you as it was for me and the ladies I taught on that day.

Why do the Roman soldiers keep lashing Him again and again with that whip?

God said: I will not do anything – my Son has to take this beating for __(insert your name)___. You need a Savior.

Why doesn't Jesus do something? He is the Son of God.

God said: My Son has to take this beating for ____(insert your name)_____. You need a Savior.

They keep lashing Him over and over with that whip. Why are they hitting Him so much?

God said: They are hitting Him so much because they are spelling ___(insert your name)_____ name. Don't you see her name written in His wounds? You need a Savior.

This horrible beating was bad. But the worse was yet to come. The Roman soldiers led him to the place where He would be crucified (Mark 15:20). Jesus started out bearing His cross (John 19:17). The physical cross was likely the wooden crosspiece probably weighing approximately 30-40 pounds. But it was too much for Him to carry so He fell. Then Simon of Cyrene was compelled to bear it for Him (Mark 15:21). Together, they arrived at the place where they were going to crucify Jesus. Wine and myrrh were offered but Jesus refused. This kind of narcotic drink was usually offered to deaden the pain, but Jesus refused (Mark 15:23). Perhaps He chose this in order to experience the ordeal of crucifixion with His full senses.

I wanted to say to Jesus – Drink it. I know it tastes bad, but it works like medicine. Take the drink it helps with the pain!

But God said: I cannot take the drink – I have to take this pain for _____(insert name)_____. You need to be set free. You need a Savior.

Then the process of the crucifixion of Jesus begins (Mark 15:24-25). A crucifixion was the cruelest and most hideous punishment possible. What you are about to read is the process of the crucifixion as described by a medical doctor. Reference: *C. Truman Davis, "The Crucifixion of Jesus. The Passion of Christ from a Medical Point of View," Arizona Medicine 22, no. 3 March 1965: 186-87, as quoted in The Expositor's Bible Commentary Vol. 8, ed. by Frank Gaebelein ([1984] pp. 779-80.*

Again, let me give you more instructions. As you read this component move to a place in your home that in case you fall, you will not hurt yourself!

. . . Simon was ordered to place the cross beam on the ground, and Jesus was quickly thrown backwards with His shoulders against the wood. A soldier felt for the depression at the front of the wrist. He drove the heavy, square, wrought-ironed nail through the wrist and deep into the wood.

I yell: God, please make them stop! Can't you see they are hurting Your Son!!

> **But God said: ___(insert your name)_____ , I love you so much I sent Jesus to take this suffering. Why? Because you needed a Savior.**

Quickly, the soldier moved to the other side to repeat the action, being careful not to pull Jesus' arms too tightly, but to allow some flexing and movement.

I wanted to yell: NO!! You cannot do this to Him. Look at how you are hurting the Son of God.

> **But Jesus whispered to me in a voice that I could hardly hear: ____(insert your name)_____ - - It's O.K. I can take the nails. Why? Because you need a Savior.**

The left foot is now pressed backward against the right foot. With both feet extended, toes down, a nail is driven through the arch of each, leaving the knees moderately flexed.

Jesus is now crucified.

Jesus slowly sags down with more weight on the nails and the wrists, excruciating, fiery pain shoots along the fingers and up the arms to explode in the brain - the nails in the wrists are putting pressure on the nerves in His hand.

I want to yell at the soldiers – take Him down. He is in so much pain!

> **But God says: No, ____(insert your name)_____.**
> **He has to stay on the cross. You need a Savior.**

     Jesus pushes Himself upward to avoid this stretching torment. He places His full weight on the nail through His feet. Again there is searing agony of the nail tearing through the nerves and the bones of the feet. At this point, His arms grow so tired and great waves of cramps sweep over the muscles, knotting them in deep, relentless throbbing pain. With these cramps, Jesus can no longer push Himself upward. Air can be drawn into the lungs, but cannot be exhaled. It's like someone has a plastic bag over his head or a pillow on His face, smothering Him to death.

I want to yell, "Breathe Jesus Breathe!!"

> **But God says: He must take a last breath _____(insert your**
> **name)_____ because you need a Savior.**

     Jesus fights to raise Himself in order to get even one small breath. Finally carbon dioxide builds up in the lungs and in the blood stream and the cramps partially subside. He is able to push Himself upward to exhale and bring in the life-giving oxygen. For 3 hours, Jesus is in limitless pain; cycles of twisting, joint-cramps, intermittent partial asphyxiation, searing torture as tissue is torn from His lacerated back as He moves up and down against the rough wood of the cross.

I see Him fighting for physical life. I know that He came for me but I do not want Him to suffer like this. I yell, "God just take Him! Do not let Him suffer.

> **But God says __(insert your name)____ He must suffer for the strength you need.**

Then another agony begins. A deep crushing pain deep in the chest. It slowly fills with serum and begins to compress the heart. It is now almost over--the loss of tissue fluids has reached a critical level - the compressed heart is struggling to pump heavy, thick, sluggish blood into the tissues - the tortured lungs are making a frantic effort to gasp in small gulps of air. *Jesus can feel the chill of death creeping through His tissues.*

His mission has been completed.

He laid down His life for us.

Finally He can allow His body to die.

It is finished – now Jesus is dead.

✿

THERE IS POWER IN THE CROSS OF CHRIST

He redeemed you with His blood. There is power over sin at the cross. God wants you to come to the cross today ladies. The question that God asks us all this morning – Are we going to accept the freedom that His Son paid so dearly for? Are we going to accept the freedom that His Son was beaten for? Are we going to accept the healing that He was beaten so badly for? If so, then come to the cross right now. There is power in the Cross of Christ that, sad to say, many Christians don't experience. Now you can learn to see Jesus' suffering and death not as some spectacle or theatrical production, but as a blueprint for how to live your life.

✐

THE MAGNITUDE OF THE CROSS

The lesson above was not just for the ladies that day. It was for the ministry within Saundra as well. This lesson forced me to slow down. It forced me to really think about the magnitude of the cross. My inner ministry and character had to be re-defined by the words of Jesus in Luke 9:23. I would like you to read this verse in several versions as I did when I studied.

Then He said to them all, "If anyone desires to come after Me, let him deny himself, and take up his cross daily, and follow Me" (Luke 9:23 NKJV).

Then he told them what they could expect for themselves: "Anyone who intends to come with me has to let me lead. You're not in the driver's seat—I am. Don't run from suffering; embrace it. Follow me and I'll show you how. Self-help is no help at all. Self-sacrifice is the way, my way, to finding yourself, your true self. What good would it do to get everything you want and lose you, the real you? If any of you is embarrassed with me and the way I'm leading you, know that the Son of Man will be far more embarrassed with you when he arrives in all his splendor in company with the Father and the holy angels. This isn't, you realize, pie in the sky by and by. Some who have taken their stand right here are going to see it happen, see with their own eyes the kingdom of God." (Luke 9:23 - 27 The Message Bible).

And He said to all, If any person wills to come after Me, let him deny himself [disown himself, forget, lose sight of himself and his own interests, refuse and give up himself] and take up his cross daily and follow Me [cleave steadfastly to Me, conform wholly to My example in living and, if need be, in dying also] (Luke 9:23 Amplified Bible).

This scripture forced me to ask myself these questions:

- *Am I willing to deny myself for the call on my life?*
- *Am I willing to be completely obedient for the call on my life?*
- *Am I willing to die for the call on my life?*

When I understood the crucifixion story in a more meaningful way, it became possible for me to *respond "yes"* to each of these questions. Experiencing the power of the cross makes it possible for me to *live "yes"* to each of these questions. I could not *live "yes"* until the ministry within had taken place! It was all a circular lesson that God was teaching me. First, God had to do a work within me so that self-denial and obedience could change my character. And then, God had to take me deeper into understanding the cross beyond knowing that He died for me. So you see, when you are called to ministry, the Cross must mean something substantive to you. When you give your life to Christ, your life is truly no longer your own. You know you belong to God. Yet, you must also know that those that you are called to minister to, must see a life of self-denial and obedience. These elements no longer become a sacrifice; they become a way of life. When the ministry within you takes place, you can begin to help others to live life abundantly (John 10:10) by experiencing the power of the cross.

When you completely understand this message, operating in victory becomes a way of life for you. You no longer operate as if you are always in a continuous spiritual battle. You recognize that the ultimate battle was won at the cross. It is the power of the cross that exposes those things that are religious and self-righteous. When you live the message of the power of the cross, you will live in dominion (Genesis 1:28), you will operate in God's power (John 8:32) and you will exercise the authority God has given to you (Luke 10:19). The gospel of Jesus Christ is the truth that has given me complete freedom in Christ. When I understood what God was saying to me all these years, the ministry God called me to do literally became a part of me. Ministry was more than just my passion; it became a part of my person. T.E.A.C.H. was no longer an acronym. The words **T**each and **E**ducate for **A**ctive **C**hristlike **H**oliness became the call of God on my life!

✐

THE FINAL QUESTION – "IS IT I?"

Before this book was sent to print, a friend of mine preached a sermon from the scripture Mark 14:17-26. A critical question was asked in verse 19. Jesus explains how one of the disciples will betray Him. And the disciples begin to sorrowfully ask, *"Is it I?"*

As I sat in the pew listening to this powerful word from the Lord, I had to ask myself, "Is it I?" I was not asking myself this question because I felt I was going to betray God or all of a sudden become corrupt. I never want my conduct to blaspheme God (Titus 2:5). But I asked myself "Is it I?" to make sure that my heart continued to remain at a humble place for ministry. A change of heart is the centerpiece of one's ministry within. I can not let anything in my life come between what Jesus did on the cross for me. So when, I ask, *"Is it I?"*, I am questioning whether or not there is anything within me that would keep me from the call and purpose for my life. Embedded in that call is my relationship with God. Embedded in that relationship is my intimacy with God. Embedded in that intimacy is who I am in Christ.

I trust that, after all these chapters on character development, major/minor tests and the power of the cross, you are better prepared to experience the ministry within. Accepting the call of God on your life will cost you everything. When we release everything that we are so that the ministry within can take place, God will do amazing things in our life and ministry. Before reading the final chapter, I would like you to meditate on the following scripture:

We are confident of all this because of our great trust in God through Christ. 5 It is not that we think we are qualified to do anything on our own. Our qualification comes from God. 6 He has enabled us to be ministers of his new covenant. This is a covenant not of written laws, but of the Spirit. The old written covenant ends in death; but under the new covenant, the Spirit gives life. (2 Corinthians 3:4-6 New Living Translation)

CHAPTER NINE

Moving Forward

This final chapter will be shorter than the others, but it is my hope that you will read fewer words from me so that you will be empowered to do more work for yourself. Having covered the subject of character, development, tests, the cross, and self-examination, this book wouldn't be complete without some practical principles to guide you as you move forward into ministry. So in the first section of this chapter, I want to discuss the subject of stewardship. Why? Because many ministers forget that our ministries do not belong to us. We desire to be successful in ministry—and in the beginning, we do pretty good. But all too often, we find it difficult to maintain the responsibility that effective ministry entails. This has been my observation and my experience. After the initial sermon, we are on fire for the Lord and we're running for our lives, but toward the middle of the journey—when the going truly gets tough—we experience discouragement and exhaustion on a whole new level. So we give up, or we feel as if we were never called to do this kind of work in the first place. This chapter will be a constant reminder to those who need to be refreshed in order to move forward. That's why I need to discuss what it means to be a steward of the ministry to which God has called you to live out. Then, I will transition a bit and share 14 of my personal yet practical strategies for maintaining the ministry within. You can buy a new car today, but you know and I know, that at some point, that car will need mainte-nance. In ministry, this same principle applies. When you begin to go through trials and your spiritual "check engine light" comes on, you can't just go out and buy a new automobile. You've got to learn how to maintain your inner ministry, or else you'll end up spiritually bankrupt.

This is why I've titled this chapter "Moving Forward." I don't just want you to move like Saundra. I want you to move forward in ministry as God would have you to move. Ultimately, it is my heart's desire that these strategies will guide you and bless you as you read them, but I do not want you to adopt them as "your" own. God ministers to every minister in a differ-ent way. What works for me may not necessarily work for you. Therefore, what I am providing is only a template. The strategies you may need, however, will be tailored for your individual "min-istry within." As you deepen your relationship with God, He will reveal your ministry-specific strategies for moving forward.

ℒ❦

WHAT IS STEWARDSHIP?

The term "stewardship" could mean many things for many peo-ple, but when I use this word, I am talking about the *supervision of something, especially the careful and responsible management of something entrusted into one's care. If we are to understand stewardship in light of our ministries, then we must first have a clear understanding of what stewardship is and what it is not. Just* like everything else, if we understand how this term applies to our life, it will change the way we make decisions each day. It will change the way we do the work of ministry, because being a good steward reflects who we are on the inside.

"For where your treasure is, there will your heart be also." Matthew 6:21

If you are a good steward, then your heart is in it. Your care is in it. Your responsibility is in it. Your investments are in it. Your concerns are in it. God desires ministers who will truly give their whole selves to the call He has placed on our lives. Being a steward of the call is one responsibility that should not be taken lightly. It is our responsibility to maintain it, and God's responsibility to help us with it. If you look at the foundation of this notion of stewardship, you will understand the strategies more clearly.

Luke 12:35 - 48
35 "Be dressed for service and keep your lamps burning, 36 as though you were waiting for your master to return from the wedding feast. Then you will be ready to open the door and let him in the moment he arrives and knocks. 37 The servants who are ready and waiting for his return will be rewarded. I tell you the truth, he himself will seat them, put on an apron, and serve them as they sit and eat! 38 He may come in the middle of the night or just before dawn. But whenever he comes, he will reward the servants who are ready. 39 "Understand this: If a homeowner knew exactly when a burglar was coming, he would not permit his house to be broken into. 40 You also must be ready all the time, for the Son of Man will come when least expected." 41 Peter asked, "Lord, is that illustration just for us

or for everyone?" 42 And the Lord replied, "A faithful, sensible servant is one to whom the master can give the responsibility of managing his other household servants and feeding them. 43 If the master returns and finds that the servant has done a good job, there will be a reward. 44 I tell you the truth, the master will put that servant in charge of all he owns. 45 But what if the servant thinks, 'My master won't be back for a while,' and he begins beating the other servants, partying, and getting drunk? 46 The master will return unannounced and unexpected, and he will cut the servant in pieces and banish him with the unfaithful. 47 "And a servant who knows what the master wants, but isn't prepared and doesn't carry out those instructions, will be severely punished. 48 But someone who does not know, and then does something wrong, will be punished only lightly. When someone has been given much, much will be required in return; and when someone has been entrusted with much, even more will be required.

This scripture passage is a familiar parable. The primary context is all about Jesus informing the disciples to be ready for the Lord's coming. In other words, He reminds them (and us) that if we have heard the gospel, then we will be held accountable to live accordingly. But like all scripture, we can apply this principle to every area of our lives. In fact, when I first heard this scripture in relationship to stewardship, it suddenly became alive to me. I began to hear God speaking to me in a new way. As I read the last few words: *"and when someone has been entrusted with much, more will be required,"* I realized the large magnitude of God's trust. First of all, He's given us a responsibility of stewardship over the call. Second of all, He's blessed us with abundant life, material possessions, marital responsibilities, and so much more. So, the self-examination question became: Am I (Saundra) being a good steward of the call, or am I simply using it as a trophy to maneuver authority?

This is a question you must answer as well, if you intend to move forward and make an impact for the sake of the kingdom.

◇

WHAT ARE WE STEWARDS OVER?

In general, we are stewards over everything God has given to us. Our schedule, our money, our gifts and abilities, our influence—it all comes from God. More specifically, our time, our talents, our treasures, our temple (body), and our testimony—none of it is ours, technically speaking. They are not our gifts. They are not our talents. Our body doesn't even belong to us (1 Corinthians 3:16, 17; I Corinthians 6:19). God has, in a sense, loaned them to us. Nothing belongs to us because we did not create our wealth, we are not owners of our health, and we certainly aren't in control over our job or family makeup. Therefore, as stewards of something that doesn't belong to us, God expects us to responsibly manage these resources in a way that pleases Him.

When I think about my own life and all the different components that God has entrusted to me, I can only fall down and worship God for trusting me with so much! I am a wife, a mother, a sister, an aunt, a daughter, a minister, an elder, a teacher, a supervisor, and a friend. He's given me gifts of teaching/administration. He's entrusted me with a vision for ministry, He's given me ideas to help other women, and every day, He's downloading more creative plans to advance the kingdom of God. God has also given me certain levels of influence on my job, which allows me to make executive decisions that others cannot make. My point is this: everything that I am, God has entrusted it to me. He has blessed me in great abundance, but at the same time, He expects me to remain grounded, and live out my calling as a steward over that which He has given me.

Consider these Scripture passages:

1 Chronicles 29: 11-13 (NLT)
11 Yours, O LORD, is the greatness, the power, the glory, the victory, and the majesty. Everything in the heavens and on earth is yours, O LORD, and this is your kingdom. We adore you as the one who is over all things. 12 Wealth and honor come from you alone, for you rule over everything. Power and might are in your hand, and at your discretion people are made great and given strength. 13 "O our God, we thank you and praise your glorious name!

Psalm 24:1 (KJV)
The earth is the LORD'S, and the fullness thereof; the world, and they that dwell therein.
☙

GROUND YOUR STRATEGIES IN THE WORD

Let's transition now to discuss the strategies I spoke about earlier. As I said previously, the strategies that God gives us ministers will always guide your stewardship, and your stewardship will be revealed through your strategies. The cycle just continues and continues until you become more equipped to carry out, on a consistent basis, what God has called you to do.

Now, first things first: your strategies must be grounded

in the word of God. The scriptures are our foundation for life's strategies. In order to live them out, the Word must become alive in you. They are not only what you believe, but your foundation scriptures are the basis for who you are in Christ. My experiences have helped me to understand who I am in Christ; and these experiences have also defined God's strategies for my ministry within. If you desire for God to reveal your strategies for moving forward, I suggest you look through your rolodex of experiences. I guarantee you, God is speaking through them. Let me share a few with you so that my strategies make more sense.

1. I have experienced spiritual warfare personally, but now, I do not run from it because I know that "no weapon formed against me can prosper." (Isaiah 54:17a)

2. I have experienced the spirit of intimidation personally, but now, I know according to the Scriptures, that "I am the head and not the tail." (Deuteronomy 28:13)

3. I have experienced true sacrifice for the sake of this ministry. I know now that there is a price that one must pay for the anointing on his or her life. Everybody says they want to be anointed, but if you want the anointing of God, it is going to cost you something. (Luke 9:23)

4. I have experienced the power of the tongue. I know now that "life and death are in the power of the tongue." Therefore, I commit to speaking life. (Proverbs 18:21; Matthew 8:8)

5. I have experienced the reward of obedience to the word

of God. When I am obedient, God promises to bless me with the good of the land. (Isaiah 1:19; 1 Samuel 15:22)

6. I have experienced the unconditional love of God. Now that I am sold out for Christ, I know that absolutely nothing can separate me from the love of God. (Romans 8:31-39).

So you see, my individual "ministry within" is developed and nurtured because of the experiences of life. Some may call these experiences "just living life," but I choose to view them as tests and trials for the betterment of God's character in me. Tests and trials will always teach you something that will ultimately produce a testimony. In these experiences, God revealed so much about His divine character, and now on a practical level, I am able to apply these foundational scriptures in my life every day. Here are the ingredients God has revealed to me. In order for me to move forward, I must include these strategies into my daily routine as a minister of His word. God instructed me to:

STRATEGY #1 – PRAY.

STRATEGY #2 – LOSE MY VOICE SO THAT I COULD SPEAK GOD'S WORD.

STRATEGY #3 – OBEY GOD'S WORD BY ANY MEANS NECESSARY.

STRATEGY #4 – ENCOURAGE MYSELF.

STRATEGY #5 – BE COMFORTABLE BEING UNCOMFORTABLE.

STRATEGY #6 – WAIT ON THE LORD.

STRATEGY #7 – STAY TRUE TO THE TEACHING OF THE WORD.

STRATEGY #8 – CULTIVATE GOD'S PRESENCE IN MY LIFE.

STRATEGY #9 – ADD ACTION TO MY FAITH.

STRATEGY #10 – PRACTICE THE SPIRITUAL DISCIPLINES.
STRATEGY #11 – LEARN TO HEAR GOD'S VOICE.
STRATEGY #12 – STAY DEEPLY GROUNDED IN THE WORD OF GOD.
STRATEGY #13 – ASSOCIATE WITH THE ANOINTING.
STRATEGY #14 – BE MOTIVATED BY LOVE.

In the next book (if the Lord delays his coming), I will discuss these strategies in more detail but remember, the list above is always evolving. This is how God spoke to the ministry within me. Fundamentally, there is nothing on this menu from which other ministers cannot benefit. But now is the time for each of you to look deep inside yourselves in order to see yourself as God sees you.

> *Be honest with yourself.*
> *Allow God to speak to you about you.*
> *This experience can transform you.*
> *It did me.*

This encounter with God changed me such that my character now reflects that of humility and obedience. It is my constant desire and prayer before the Lord: "keep me humble, and help me to obey you." In order for God to use you, He must constantly transform you to His image. Now that your inner ministry is more developed, you are now ready to "PREACH THE WORD!!!"

CLOSING THOUGHT FOR MEDITATION

Don't become so well-adjusted to your culture that you fit into it without even thinking. Instead, fix your attention on God. You'll be changed from the inside out. Readily recognize what He wants from you, and quickly respond to it. Unlike the culture around you, always dragging you down to its level of immaturity, God brings the best out of you, develops well-formed maturity in you. (Romans 12:2 The Message Bible)

ACKNOWLEDGMENTS

With all my heart I would like to say thank you and I love you to some very important people in my life:

My Pastor Bishop L. Foday and First Lady Kay Farrar and the Solid Rock Ministry International Family

My mentor, Dr. Shirley R. Brown and the Destiny International Ministries Family

The Philadelphia Community, Rockingham, North Carolina

The T.E.A.C.H. Faculty and Staff and all the ladies who support T.E.A.C.H.

The T.E.A.C.H. Intercessors, who constantly undergird me with prayer

The Ladies I mentor - who are why The Ministry Within is so important

Dr. Christine Grant and Mrs. Shinica Thomas, who are the "wind beneath my wings"

Deacon Ervin and Mrs. Magnolia Jones, our Family Care Leaders

Shaun and Ana Saunders, Godzchild Productions, Inc.

Jonathan McDougald, J. Alexander Online

Regent University School of Divinity Faculty and Staff
The North Carolina Community College System (H. Martin Lancaster, former president and R. Scott Ralls, current president)

My wonderful Kappa Omicron Chapter of Alpha Kappa Alpha Sorority, Inc. Line Sisters – Fall 1984

The Black Women Investment Corporation
The people who make it possible for me to minister as they are always there whenever we need them for anything: Willie, Carol, Courtney, and Crystal Clark; Tim, Latitia, Jasmine, Timia and Carrington Rodgers; Grady and Wanda Bussey; Pebbles Farrar; James and Beverly Gaither; Cralg, Monya, Joseph and Sarah James; Minister Katie Dunston; Martha Freeman (with her wonderful husband the late Deacon Bill Freeman); Deacon William and Mary Mangum; Candace Thomas, and all my cousins from Rockingham.

To my wonderful friend, the beautiful lady who for over 15 years always took the time to make sure I was always "ready": The late Nancy Kelly of Visions Hair Salon. I miss her so much!! Nancy's daughter, Shonda Gunnell is now carrying on!

Finally, special thanks to the lady who titled my first book – Catina Clemons. She told me one day after church to keep it simple - just call the book "The Ministry Within" because that's what it's all about! Thanks Catina!

About the Author

C♥

Dr. Saundra Wall Williams is the founder of T.E.A.C.H. (Teach and Educate for Active Christlike Holiness™), Inc. in Raleigh, North Carolina. She is indeed a woman of excellence and action whom God has chosen for ministry to teach, preach, speak and write to the spiritual needs of women. She is a powerful speaker who has dedicated her life and ministry to teaching so that others can move to active Christlike holiness.

Through the direction of the Holy Spirit and the covering of her pastor, Dr. Williams has established T.E.A.C.H., Inc. The mission of T.E.A.C.H. is to equip and encourage women for their life and ministry calling through a holistic teaching approach. T.E.A.C.H. is working to maximize the ministry potential of women all over the world in God's Word. This mission is accomplished through dynamic and anointed seminars, study materials, small group study sessions, conferences, retreats, and mentoring. Headquartered in Raleigh, NC, T.E.A.C.H. concentrates on TEACHing™ in SPIRIT and in TRUTH.

Dr. Williams received her call to the ministry in 1996 and was licensed in the gospel ministry in 2000, and was ordained as Elder in the Full Gospel Baptist Church Fellowship in 2005. She stands as an obedient, yielded woman of God. In doing the work of the Kingdom, Saundra is the Elder of Christian Education at Solid Rock Ministry International in Garner, NC where Bishop L. Foday Farrar, Bishop of Global Affairs for the Full Gospel Baptist Church Fellowship, is her Pastor. In this role, she is responsible for all adult education at SRMI. She was recently appointed by District Overseer Luther Brooks as the District Director of Christian Education for the Full Gospel Baptist Church Fellowship International Central District.

Dr. Williams is currently the Sr. Vice-President and Chief of Technology and Workforce Development for the North Carolina Community College System. Before coming to the Community College System, she was a professor at North Carolina State University and prior to that, worked 13 years in business and industry in the areas of information technology and training. She holds a Bachelor of Science in Mathematics, Master of Science in Applied Mathematics and Statistics and a Doctor of Education in Adult and Community College Education from North Carolina State University. She also holds a Master of Divinity from Regent University. She is also a certified Christian Coach, where her specialty area is women in ministry. She feels that her professional and educational achievements were only preparation for God's Kingdom building assignments.

Dr. Williams was born in Rockingham, NC and is the daughter of Mr. Leon Wall, Sr. and Mrs. Pauline Patterson Wall. She is a 1981 graduate from Richmond Senior High School. Saundra is married to Mr. Dennis O. Williams and they celebrate 21 years of marriage. God has blessed them with one son, Bradley Joseph.

Dr. Williams knows that the Word of God for the calling on her life and ministry comes from Matthew 6:33, *"But seek first the kingdom of God and His righteousness, and all these things shall be added to you."*

CONTACT DR. SAUNDRA
WALL WILLIAMS

ℒ❧

Speaking Engagements and Ordering The Ministry Within
Contact Dr. Williams through her website or by mail:
www.teachministries.org/saundrawallwilliams

Mailing address:
Dr. Saundra Wall Williams
Post Office Box 41161
Raleigh, NC 27629

For more information about T.E.A.C.H. Conferences, online courses, webinars, seminars and mentoring visit the T.E.A.C.H. website www.teachministries.org

Also become a friend on Facebook www.facebook.com/the-teachnetwork and follow Dr. Williams on Twitter @SaundraWall-Williams

Finally, to order books or for more information about Dr. Saundra Wall Williams, you may contact her publisher, Godzchild Publications, at www.godzchildproductions.net or call toll free at 877-777-7016.